GW00383850

The Powerhouse of God

The Church –
God's Statement to the World,
to Principalities and to Powers

Johannes Facius

Sovereign World

Sovereign World Ltd
PO Box 777
Tonbridge
Kent TX11 9XT
England

ISBN: 1 85240 114 1

Typeset by CRB Associates, Lenwade, Norwich
Printed in England by Clays Ltd, St. Ives plc

Contents

Chapter 1

Why God Created the Church

If we want to understand the function and the role of the Church, we must first of all come to know why God created her. This is important because in God's creational purposes for the Church lies the understanding of how she should function in this world.

Our usual perception of the calling of the Church is that she is in this world in order to preach the Gospel. And although this is certainly part of God's purpose, it is far from being all, nor is it the most important calling of the Church.

We must try not to 'humanize' the Church too much. By this I mean that we must not consider the Church from a worldly point of view, as if it were just some other human organisation that should be run like any other business. It is true to say that Christians today often have forgotten about the spiritual nature of the Church, which is why we focus so much on human activity; on making the Church efficient according to worldly concepts. But God's purpose is far deeper or far higher than that.

The Church is, first and foremost, an eternal entity. Therefore, its existence is not limited to time, space and history. It is eternal and will go on to exist forever.

A Testimony to the Powers of Darkness

In the oldest book in the Bible, we find an illustration of God's purpose for the Church: the mystery of Job's sufferings and final triumph.

In God's dealings with Job we see some of His eternal purposes revealed. It is in line with good theology to use Old Testament individuals as illustrations of God's purposes for His New Testament Church, bearing in mind the fundamental differences between the Old and the New Testament. During the time of the Old Covenant, God was dealing with individual persons, whereas when the New Covenant is introduced, God's focus is on a corporate being; the Church, or the body of Christ. However, the eternal purposes are the same. What God wanted to prove through His servant Job is the same as what He wants to prove through His New Testament Church.

There are those who claim that Job's sufferings were due to his sins, and that his deliverance and restoration came through his confession at the very end. To me, such a view is not only a misconception of what really happened, but it is also a misreading of the text.

Job did not suffer because he had sinned. He suffered because he had not sinned and, therefore, could be used as a testimony against the devil. The first chapter of the book of Job proves this beyond any doubt. Read verses 6–12: it was God who took the initiative to challenge Satan with His servant. So, this story of such great pain and suffering was not initiated by the devil, but by the Lord, and through all the unhappy events with his family, Job gets this testimony:

> *'In all this Job did not sin nor charge God with wrong.'*
> (Job 1:22)

God challenged Satan not with Job's sins, but with his righteousness, saying:

> *'Have you considered My servant Job, that there is none like him on the earth, a blameless and upright man, one who fears God and shuns evil?'*   (Job 2:3)

Job, therefore, did not fall into Satan's power because of his sins, but because God allowed His work in that man to be severely tested. In other words: God wanted to use Job as an instrument to prove Satan wrong! He wanted the adversary to realize that all his efforts to destroy God's work and God's plan with His redeemed people had been to no avail. God had triumphed in the human flesh.

There was and is no need for God to prove that He in Himself is victorious. The devil already knows that. Everybody in the spiritual world realizes that. The battle is over God's creation. The conflict is between man and the devil. Can it be proven and manifested that all the consequences of man's fall can be overcome? That is what the story of Job is all about, and that is what the life of the Church is all about. As the redeemed community of people on earth, God wants us to prove that His finished work in redeeming us from our sins and restoring us from the fall has fully triumphed over all evil. We are to be God's living testimony that Jesus has totally and fully overcome the works of Satan!

A Testimony into the Unseen Realm

This underlines that the calling of the Church is not primarily to the physical realm, but to be a testimony to the spiritual world. That is what Paul refers to in his statement in Ephesians 3:10–11:

> *'to the intent that now the manifold wisdom of God might be made known by the church to the principalities and powers in the heavenly places, according to the eternal purpose which He accomplished in Christ Jesus our Lord.'*

This means that the Church has a calling to prove something in front of the principalities and powers in the heavenlies. We are not just here to be a testimony to secular society. We exist as the Church for God's purposes within the spiritual realm. And what He needs us for is this: that everything He accomplished in Christ Jesus on the cross may be displayed in its full reality!

That is the meaning also of 'being His witnesses'. Notice this expression. It comes from Acts 1:8 and is well known, perhaps especially, to all Pentecostal and Charismatic people in the Church. However, it remains a question whether we have really understood what this means. We tend to interpret it as being empowered to be able to witness for Christ; that is to have boldness to talk about the gospel before men. But that is not what it says: it says that we are to **be** witnesses, not to **do** witnessing! The power of the Holy Spirit was given in order to enable us to become a living testimony about Jesus, to carry and to manifest His character and His life, not just to have a loose tongue. It is what we are that determines whether we can prove God's victory, not what we say or what we do!

It was Job's righteousness that was the challenge, not his Charismatic gifts or his actions. William Shakespeare's famous quote wasn't: 'To do or not to do! That is the question!' No, he wrote: 'To be or not to be! That is the question!' And that really is the question when we speak about the calling of the Church.

The Light of the World

When Jesus spoke about the calling of the Church to His disciples, He described it like this:

> *'You are the light of the world. A city that is set on a hill cannot be hidden. . . . Let your light so shine before men, that they may see your good works and glorify your Father in heaven.'* (Matthew 5:14 & 16)

The question here is what would, in fact, constitute the light? Did Jesus say: 'Let your wonderful singing be heard'? Or 'Let your perfect doctrines be exposed'? Or 'Let your fantastic church-organisation be shown'? All of this may be good and necessary, but it is not *the light of this world'*. The light is behaviour: *'Let them see your good works and glorify your Father in heaven'*! It points to the kind of life we are living as believers, and the kind of character we are manifesting.

What impresses the world is not signs and wonders, high-profiled evangelism, dynamic faith-actions or any other expression of the Charismatic gifts. All this is good and wonderful, but it does not leave any lasting impact upon secular society. Only the manifestation of the character and spirit of Jesus can be the light of the world. That is why the Lord Jesus Himself prayed in His last prayer,

> *'that they all may be one, . . . that the world may believe, that You sent Me.'* (John 17:21)

It was the love between the brethren, the care for one another, the showing forth of the fruit of the Spirit that was to convince the world about the reality of the gospel.

Jesus' words about being the light of the world conclude His teaching on the beatitudes in the beginning of Matthew 5:

> *'Blessed are the poor in spirit, . . . Blessed are those who mourn, . . . Blessed are the meek, . . . the merciful, . . . the pure in heart, . . . the peacemakers, . . . those who are persecuted for righteousness' sake.'* (Matthew 5:3–10)

All are a manifestation of the character of the Lamb of God. Tongues, prophecy, faith, signs and wonders, healing and power-evangelism are all good things, but none of the gifts constitute *'the light of the world'*; only the revealing of the nature and personality of Jesus in and through His disciples and His Church will achieve this.

9

A Corporate Light

This was meant to be a corporate expression, not an expression by individual people only. That is why the Lord says in talking about being the light of the world:

> *'A city that is set on a hill cannot be hidden.'*
>
> (Matthew 5:14)

A city is a community of people who are living together in a common life. So, it is the relationships between the members of the body, displayed in unity and love, that is the light of this world. No single person can fully express the glory of the Lord Jesus. We can all individually reflect some aspect of His majestic character, but only together living as a body can we show forth to the world who Jesus Christ really is.

We need to come back to this understanding, as we live in a time where the emphasis has been centered so much on the individual. In my opinion, we as Charismatic people, who claim to have experienced the baptism of the Holy Spirit, have not really understood the ultimate purpose of the Pentecostal experience. In many ways, we have stopped short of the real thing by dwelling too much on the signs of this experience. It is true that there are signs of tongues and prophecy and miraculous manifestations to follow this event, but the real goal is to establish us in living as a body. Therefore the true outcome of the day of Pentecost is found not in the beginning, but in the end of the second chapter of Acts:

> *'Now all who believed were together, and had all things in common, and sold their possessions and goods, and divided them among all, as anyone had need. So continuing daily with one accord in the temple, and breaking bread from house to house, they ate their food with gladness and simplicity of heart, praising God and having favor with all the people. And the Lord added to the church daily those who were being saved.'*
>
> (Acts 2:44–47)

A People Bearing the Fruits of the Gospel

> *'... that they may see your good works and glorify your Father in heaven.'* (Matthew 5:16)

The apostle Peter has something to say along this theme. He defines the nature of the Church like this:

> *'But you are a chosen generation, a royal priesthood, a holy nation, His own special people, that you may proclaim the praises of Him who called you out of darkness, into His marvelous light.'* (1 Peter 2:9)

This is the text from the New King James, and the phrase 'proclaim His praises' could easily be misunderstood, in the sense that we could think that we could represent Jesus by our mouth in 'telling' or 'singing' His praises. The good old King James leaves us with no chance of mistakes: *'that ye should shew forth the virtues of Him.'* We are called to manifest the virtues, the character of Him, and if we do not do that, all our 'proclaiming' is useless anyway. The world has no problem differentiating between word and deed.

The reason why God created the Church can be expressed in a nutshell: He wanted to show Himself to the world!

The writer to the Hebrews describes a radical change in God's way of communicating in the first chapter of his letter to the Hebrews:

> *'... God, who at various times and in various ways spoke in time past to the fathers by the prophets, has in these last days spoken to us by His Son, ... who being the brightness of His glory and the express image of His person...'* (Hebrews 1:1–3)

In times past, God chose to speak to men through the oracles of prophets. That is the Old Testament way of communicating, but that has changed radically since the introduction of the New Covenant.

Now God speaks through His Son and His body, the Church (including prophetic gifts), and the way He speaks is no longer just the oracles of men. He basically speaks by revealing His Son in human flesh. Just as the great invisible God manifests Himself through Jesus, who reflects the brightness of His glory and the image of His person, so the Son now speaks through manifesting His character and person through His body, the Church. Ministry under the New Covenant is therefore very different from Old Covenant ministry. It is no longer a matter of communicating words by speaking, but that of communicating life and spirit. For that reason the New Testament uses extraordinary words to describe the nature of ministry.

In 2 Corinthians 3:18, Paul describes us as being mirrors reflecting the glory of the Lord as we behold Him and are being transformed into the same image. In the previous chapter of the same letter, he speaks about us being censers spreading the fragrance of Christ as an aroma, bringing life to those who are being saved, and death to those who are perishing.

And then again, in chapter 3, he talks about being epistles of Christ, written not with ink but by the Spirit of the living God. Reflecting mirrors, smelling censers and living epistles, communicating the life of Christ in the Holy Spirit to impact the lives of people and to prove to the unseen world that God has indeed triumphed through the cross of Jesus in the lives of the redeemed people of God.

Chapter 2

Unity is Crucial

If we are to be God's proof in both the spiritual and the physical realm that Jesus has won the victory over all sin and restored all that was lost in the fall, then the whole matter of the unity of Christ's body becomes absolutely crucial.

How can a divided Church ever prove the victory of the cross, when the very sin of all sins is division, or separation? Through the fall (of sin) man was separated from his God and Creator, and through the same fall he was also separated from his brother. Can a divided and crippled Body of Christ ever prove anything, let alone reflect the glory of the risen Lord? Did not the Lord utter in His great high-priestly prayer in the garden, that He had given His people God's glory in order that they might be one?

That really means that God's glory is forever closely linked with the unity of His Church. If there is unity, then there is glory and if there is no unity, then the glory of God has departed.

What is God's glory? It is not some kind of charismatic emotion that we can feel when we are together as God's people. God's glory is Christ, none other and nothing else. When Christ is revealed, we encounter God's glory. Where Christ is not being manifested in the body, any talk about seeing or feeling the glory is nothing but charismatic 'hocus pocus'. He, Christ, is the brightness of God's glory that we read about in Hebrews 1:3. A divided, disagreeing Body of Christ has no way of reflecting God's glory. Thus, unity becomes crucial in order for the Church to fulfill its calling.

The Church must be able to prove that the main sin of separation and division has been overcome. Otherwise, we have no legal or moral foundation for exercising our God-given authority over the powers of darkness nor any credibility to proclaim the truth of the Gospel in the world.

This fact was brought home to me many years ago when I was working as an evangelist in Denmark. We were conducting a gospel campaign in a small town and would go out into the streets to witness for the Lord and hand out tracts. This little town had quite a few churches, which were almost all located on the main street. During this campaign, I met a young man one night, and as we talked, I did my best to present to him the Gospel. I shared with him about the love of the Lord and ended by promising him that if he would, indeed, give his life to the Lord he would become a member of a wonderful family of believers. He looked very interested at first, but then said that he had a couple of questions.

First of all, he wondered how it really could be so wonderful to know the love of Jesus, when, apparently, those who were already His did not seem to love one another very much. Secondly, he said that if he were to become a member of this wonderful family could I please point out to him which of these many churches on the main street he should join? I was stunned and unable to carry on the conversation. I went straight back to the meeting tent, knelt down behind the platform and cried out: 'Lord, we have destroyed your testimony and undermined the credibility of your Gospel!'

However, the unity of the Church is not just crucial for the physical world. It is even more so for the unseen realm. The whole matter of spiritual warfare hinges on this point, for if the Church cannot overcome the enemy within its own midst, how can we ever hope to overcome the principalities and powers ruling in the heavenlies? If we cannot deliver the proof that Jesus has fully triumphed over the works of the devil inside the Church, how can we with any moral right make demands on Satan's bastions in the world?

Some years ago, I had the joy to participate three years in a row in the annual city-wide prayer conference in St. Louis, USA. We had a couple of hundred intercessors participating from different churches in the city, and we prayed and did spiritual warfare against what we discerned to be some of the major strongholds over the city. We especially concentrated on the issue of racism, as St. Louis is an old slave-trade center. The market-place in front of the old Town Hall had been used for slave-trading. The spirit of racism has been ruling in the hearts of many inhabitants, both white and black, since those days and has also continually affected the relationship between black and white believers.

However, I am afraid that we were not too successful in our prayers over this matter. We were all wondering after the first two years, why there seemed to have been no break-through in this area. Then, before I even left home for the third conference I had a dream one night. I very seldom have dreams. I guess being the blend of a cool Danish Viking and a level-headed German does not allow for much dreaming. So, whenever I do have a dream I usually take it quite seriously.

I dreamt I was entering the throne-room in heaven. I could see the Lord sitting there as the Judge. Then someone appeared that I understood to be the devil. He had a complaint to make. He said: 'Most High God, some of your people in St. Louis have commanded me to withdraw my powers of racism from the city. But you know, Most High God, and I know, that the hearts of your own people are full of racism. Must I then obey this command?' Then I heard the voice of the Lord replying: 'Satan, I wish it was so; that this command would have to be implemented, but as long as my own people have not dealt with the matter they have no moral right to make claims on anybody!'

When I woke up the next morning I realised that I had just come to understand something that would forever change my whole concept of spiritual warfare. If we cannot be the testimony manifesting the manifold wisdom of God in front of the principalities and powers, if we cannot prove that Jesus through His finished work on the cross has overcome the works of division in our own hearts, then we can forget all about spiritual warfare.

As I shared this with the leaders of the conference in St. Louis, I also expressed my concern over the fact that we had had no black believers with us in our two previous conferences in St. Louis. In agreement with the other leaders three of the leading black pastors were then invited to the third conference. They were asked to report about what it was like to be a black Christian in the predominantly white Body of Christ in the city. Their report was shocking and, in the end, all the white brothers and sisters in the conference were in tears. But the black pastors ended their report in a surprising way. They said that they had not come just to tell how badly they had been treated by the white part of the body. They had come to ask their white brothers and sisters to forgive them for harboring bitterness, resentment and even hatred in their hearts. Then they asked the white pastors to come up on the platform. As the broken white pastors reached the stage, they said that they needed to ask forgiveness from their black brothers and sisters for all the pain they had inflicted upon them.

It was an extraordinary meeting, and certainly one that I shall never forget until the day I die. Something broke in the spiritual realm over St. Louis that evening. I was told later that this meeting of reconciliation led to a more public manifestation where black and white members of the body met at the old slave-market in the city, holding hands while publicly confessing the sins of the past. Also, I was told that a Gospel Campaign held shortly after this event turned out to be one of the most blessed and successful outreaches in the city.

We need to realise what it means to be in Christ, to be transformed into His likeness and to reflect His life. In Galatians 3:26–27, Paul speaks about the reality of being baptized into Christ:

'For as many of you as were baptized into Christ have put on Christ. There is neither Jew nor Greek, there is neither slave nor free, there is neither male nor female; for you are all one in Christ Jesus.'

Baptism is a radical experience. It means a total conclusion of the old life. It is a funeral service for the old man. In the death of Christ, we have died to everything concerning our past life. There is no more place for nationalism, rascism, social barriers or the barrier between the sexes. This does not mean that we do not have these identities. We are still different races and peoples, and we remain either men or women, but these differences no longer separate us. There are no barriers in Jesus. Through His cross He has pulled all of them down. There is also no religious barrier. For Colossians 3:11 includes *'there is neither ... circumcised nor uncircumcised'* and also the cultural wall of separation is broken, for in Christ *'there is neither ... barbarian* [nor] *Scythian'*. If we are truly in Christ these things have all passed away. In Jesus, there are no barriers. Since the Church is in Christ, this is what she should manifest. And yet, look how we have allowed all these things of the flesh to separate us from one another. If we all lived in the reality of our baptism, unity would not be such a present problem.

The baptism of the Spirit aims at this very thing. The true evidence of being properly baptized in the Holy Spirit is not tongues or other manifestations, it is that we are able to overcome the barriers that separate us from one another.

The following is Paul's version of the Pentecostal experience:

'For by one Spirit we were all baptized into one body – whether Jews or Greeks, whether slaves or free – and have all been made to drink into one Spirit.'

(1 Corinthians 12:13)

It is clear from this that the power of the Spirit was given to us in order to empower us to be able to overcome all of our differences and live and function together in love and harmony as one body. For that reason, those who claim to have received this power ought to be the first ones to humble themselves and receive their fellow-members of the body. Sad to say this is often not so. The Pentecostal movement and the Charismatic movement belong to the most divided and split up Christian groups in the world.

Once, on one of my many travels, I came to a major city in the States. This was my first visit to that city, and so I asked my host a little about the situation of the churches. I also wanted to know which churches were represented in the city. So, he took me for a drive downtown to show me some of the local churches. 'On this corner,' he said, 'you will find a white church, and over on that corner you have a black church. And then down this street we have a Chinese church. We have also a Korean church.' And so he went on and on. I asked myself where in the New Testament do we read about 'a white church' or 'a black church'? How strange also that in an American city they have Chinese churches and Korean churches! One would have thought that the whole idea about the Church would be that the same church could consist of both white and black people and Chinese, Korean and other nationalities a well. After all, in Christ all these barriers have been removed!

God never intended for the Church to be a replica of secular society. No, he wanted her to be an example of His eternal purpose for mankind. The Church should be the light of the world, not the mirror of society! Until we acknowledge this problem and give ourselves to a true restoration of God's plan and purpose for His Church we shall remain weak in our testimony to the world and crippled in our warfare against the principalities and powers in the heavenlies.

Chapter 3

Growing up Into Maturity

Throughout the last many decades, the Holy Spirit has been at work in the Church to bring her out of her infancy and weakness and into the fullness to which God has called her.

One of the reasons for the cropping up of so many para-church organisations in the Body of Christ is, undoubtedly, that the Church has not been functioning in its fullness. Therefore, God has raised up special ministries all over the world, not just to get the job done, but even more so, I believe, to challenge the Church and to help her to mature and enter into her fullness.

It is my view that the Word of God points to the Church as God's chosen instrument. All the ministries are given for the sole purpose of equipping the saints, for their work of ministry, which is to build up and edify the Body of Christ (Ephesians 4:12). The goal is expressed in the continuation of Ephesians 4:

> 'till we all come to the unity of the faith and the know-ledge of the Son of God, to a perfect man, to the measure of the stature of the fullness of Christ; that we should no longer be children, tossed to and fro and carried about with every wind of doctrine, by the trickery of men, in the cunning craftiness by which they lie in wait to deceive, but, speaking the truth in love, may grow up in all things into Him who is the head – Christ.'
>
> (Ephesians 4:13–15)

All our efforts as ministers and ministries must be to work to the end that the body may grow up and mature, being able to fulfill its divine calling. God has chosen the body, and His plans and purposes can only be accomplished through a mature body which works and functions in unity and love.

All God's purposes and plans are suffering when the Body of Christ is not flowing in unity and maturity.

One can almost hear God's heart cry in the words of the apostle John in his first letter:

> *'I write to you, little children, because your sins are forgiven you for His name's sake. I write to you, fathers, because you have known Him, who is from the beginning. I write to you, young men, because you have overcome the wicked one.'* (1 John 2:12–13)

Three categories of people are outlined here, or three levels of spiritual maturity: the children, the youth and the fathers.

Although this, of course, is referring to three actual age-groups in the Church, I believe, that it is also an exposure of spiritual levels that we have in the Church.

We have believers who are at the children's level. Others are found to be functioning at a youthful level. And then we have the grown-ups, the fathers. Actually, we will find whole churches living at one of these three levels of maturity today.

What is characteristic for children? The apostle John says, that 'they have their sins forgiven'. In other words: children are taken up with blessings, with gifts and with whatever they can get from God. It is natural for children to be selfish, to be taken up with their own needs. There are many believers and many churches who are living at this level. Their whole focus is their needs. It is not hard to discern when you are in such a 'children's church'. The focus is on what we might get from God. You hear it when you listen to their prayers. They are all centered around getting things from the Lord. You hear it from the preaching and the teaching. It is all about knowing ways and means whereby you can get fulfilled, happy and content. One would think that people in such churches believed that God had been invented only for their needs and purposes.

Then there is the 'youthful' church. John characterizes it as 'being strong and having overcome the evil one'. This is the Church of power and action. The emphasis is on power-manifestations, on doing exploits of faith, on exercising the spiritual gifts. There is a lot of spiritual warfare going on, chasing the demons. Such churches are built and upheld on hyper-activity. The focus is on overcoming problems, attacks, sickness and weakness. If such churches should ever experience times of silence, people would react by thinking that they had lost the anointing. Faith in action is good, but we must not have our whole attention upon what must be done nor upon the works of our adversary.

'The fathers', in contrast, speaks about the mature Church. John describes the fathers as those 'who know Him, who is from the beginning'. These are the people who have come to know God and their sole focus has become the Lord Himself. All they talk about, all they sing about, all they preach about are the persons of God the Father; Christ the Son; and the Holy Spirit. There is little emphasis on what God can give, or what He can do as in the children's and the youthful Church. Here, the focus is the Lord. To know 'Him who is from the beginning' means to know God in His eternal creational purposes. To know what it was God set out for, when He created everything. To know where God's heart is, what He is after in history and throughout eternity. This is the mature Church, which has come away from the childish and selfish things and is being taken up with the kingdom of God. Oh, how God must be longing for His Church to grow up and be able to join Him in His plans and purposes.

The Responsible Church

The mark of maturity is responsibility. From a mature person you can expect that he is acting in a responsible way. The mature Church takes responsibility for God's creation.

In Romans 8, Paul states that God has a plan to redeem not only mankind, but all of His creation. He reveals that God has designated that all of creation *'will be delivered from the bondage of corruption into the glorious liberty of the children of God'* (Romans 8:21 NKJV). Since God has such a plan for all of creation, the mature Church must engage itself to work with God accordingly, and not just be occupied with the salvation of individual souls. Let us take a closer look at this marvelous scripture, and read it more in its context:

> *'The Spirit Himself bears witness with our spirit that we are children of God, and if children, then heirs – heirs of God and joint heirs with Christ, if indeed we suffer with Him, that we might also be glorified together.*
>
> *For I consider that the sufferings of this present time are not worthy to be compared with the glory which shall be revealed in us. For the earnest expectation of the creation eagerly waits for the revealing of the sons of God.*
>
> *For the creation was subjected to futility, not willingly, but because of Him who subjected it in hope; because the creation itself also will be delivered from the bondage of corruption into the glorious liberty of the children of God. For we know that the whole creation groans and labors with birth pangs together until now.'*
>
> (Romans 8:16–22)

First of all we need to know who we are. We are *'heirs of God and joint heirs with Christ'*. Now think about this! Joint heirs with Christ! What a calling! What a privilege! But since we are heirs with Christ, we need to know what it is that we are inheriting. We are, of course, inheriting exactly what Christ is inheriting. And Christ's inheritance is that which is expressed in the second Psalm:

> *'Ask of Me, and I will give You the nations for Your inheritance, and the ends of the earth for Your posses-sion.'*   (Psalm 2:8)

The nations and the earth; that will be our inheritance together with Christ. This being so means that we ought to take great interest in what is happening among the nations and with the earth. We must learn to take responsibility for that which will be ours.

The whole of creation is in pain, groaning because it is in bondage to the corruption of sin. It is eagerly waiting for the revealing of the sons of God. The sons of God are the grown up children of God, and this is just another expression of the mature Church. All of creation is waiting for the Church to come of age, so that it can be transferred from the bondage of corruption into the glorious liberty of the children of God. This is remarkable. Creation, the nations and the earth, are not waiting for the politicians, nor for any peace plan from fallen man. It is waiting for 'the sons of God' to come forth and take over.

This is the age of the kingdom of God, where we shall reign and rule over the earth as kings and priests with Christ for a thousand years. Is it not then about time that we assume our responsibility for God's creation? I have said that the fathers, the mature Church, knows God's creational purposes from the beginning of time. According to Genesis 1:26, God's purpose in creating man was to put him in charge over the earth, and over everything that moves on it. From the beginning we were designated to rule the earth on God's behalf and in close fellowship with Him. But sin came in, and we lost our glory. This was the devil's master stroke in an attempt to take charge himself over God's creation.

Sin means that we lost our inheritance, the privilege of administrating God's work. But what was lost through sin must, of course, have been restored in redemption. What Jesus did on the cross was not only to eliminate the guilt of sin, but also to restore us back into our creational position: to rule the earth for God. The Church, God's redeemed and forgiven people, being brought back to this glorious position, must therefore assume its full responsibility.

What God has Created

What is it then that God has created for which we must bear responsibility?

People

First of all, God created people. Men, women and children, and lots of them. We are responsible for many more people outside the Church than inside it, and it would be good for us to realize that. For so long we have concentrated on our own people and our own affairs, just as if the world is of no concern to us. We are saved and on our way to heaven, and the rest of God's creation is going down the drain. If the Church is not heavily engaged in missions, evangelism and social work, it shows itself to be stuck in spiritual immaturity. We should be deeply concerned about the way people in our society are living, and we should be the first ones to reach out to them in their spiritual and physical need. It is amazing to realize how much room caring for the poor is given in the teachings and practice of both Jesus and the early Church. People are created by God and in His image, and they are our responsibility.

Nature

It is not at all wrong when Christians feel for environmental issues. This should be a natural response from all believers, and the Church, of course, should be engaging herself in the protection of God's creation. Trees, plants, animals, mountains, lakes, rivers and the sea; indeed, the very air we breathe is God's creation, which He made to bless people.

Throughout this century, mankind has systematically exploited, polluted and exhausted nature to such a degree that leading scientists tell us that within the next one hundred years we will have destroyed all natural resources, and the globe will be sinking into a global catastrophe. This is the consequence of Satan's rule through sinful men. That is why creation is groaning so much under the power of corruption. It is not meant for destruction and God will not allow it to be completely destroyed, at least not during this age. On the contrary, He has planned to restore it back to its original fruitfulness and glory.

We have the old promises that one day the earth shall be filled with the glory of the Lord as the waters cover the sea. Every mountain and every valley shall reflect the beauty of the Lord. In the New Testament, Jesus in a speech to His disciples said this:

> '. . . in the regeneration, when the Son of Man sits on the throne of His glory, you who have followed Me will also sit on twelve thrones, judging the twelve tribes of Israel.'
> (Matthew 19:28)

Notice the word 'regeneration', the same as rebirth. When the Lord Jesus comes back and establishes His glorious kingdom on earth, we shall see the regeneration of God's creation. For that reason and because we have been called to be His joint-heirs and joint-rulers we must learn to take responsibility for everything God created and to care for it.

Nations

The Bible is clear on the fact that nations are created by God. For instance Acts 17:26:

> 'And He has made from one blood every nation of men to dwell on all the face of the earth, and has determined their preappointed times and the boundaries of their dwellings.'

God is the God of the nations and He is the one who rules and forms world-history down through the ages.

If nations were not of God, why would the New Testament tell us in Matthew 25 that when Jesus comes He will assemble all the nations and judge them? God will hold the nations responsible for the way they have acted according to their God-given destiny. Also the book of Revelation states that there will be nations who are saved and who will take their place in the New Jerusalem (Revelation 21:24).

Of course, God must be deeply interested in the nations since He has called us, the Church, to go into all the world and make disciples of all the nations.

Let us remember that it was the Lord who caused the people of this earth to be divided up into many tongues and tribes at the great confusion at Babel. He did this in His love for mankind, in order to prevent them being totally destroyed through the power of sin. Acts 17:27 confirms that God arranged the nation's times and boundaries in order to draw them closer to Himself, and give them a hope of seeking Him and finding Him.

If it is true that we, as the Church, have been called to reign with Christ over the earth in the coming millennium kingdom (Revelation 1:6 and 20:6), then we must take up our responsibility now and start praying and caring for the nations of the world. For all those who overcome and are following the Lord Jesus, there is this wonderful promise:

> '*And he who overcomes, and keeps My works until the end, to him I will give power over the nations. "He shall rule them with a rod of iron; As the potter's vessels shall be broken to pieces ".'*   (Revelation 2:26–27)

Governments

It is in the same line of thought that Paul is exhorting the New Testament Church to pray for the nation. He even orders us to first of all offer up prayers and intercessions and thanksgiving for all men, for kings and for those, who are in positions of authority.

Whenever we have a people (all men), a king (or a head of state), and a government (those in authority), we have a nation. Therefore God must take a great deal of interest in nations, since He urges His Church regularly to watch over the nation in prayer. The reason for this is quite clear in 1 Timothy 2: God wants the nation to have true peace, prosperity and true salvation through His Son, the Lord Jesus, who gave His life as a ransom for all men.

Taking responsibility for the government is for many believers a difficult subject. They don't want to be involved in politics. To them, politics is dirty business, and maybe they have a point. But could it be that politics has turned out to be so dirty because the Church has been negligent in praying for the government? And could it be that we have so many bad governments in the world because we do not take responsibility for our governments in prayer and spiritual warfare?

I don't for a moment believe that God is taken up with party-politics. He is neither conservative nor socialist, and He is certainly not liberal. By 'government' we are dealing with the institution. The institution of government is created and willed by God, for without it everything would turn into chaos and people would suffer immensely.

According to Romans 13:1–7, government is from God. It is the ordinance of God and we as believers are urged to submit and obey. But it is also true that there is some qualification to go with this statement. The government which is supported by God, according to Paul, is God's minister to us for good, and God's protection for us against evil. The government that qualifies as being from God is a government which encourages good and rewards good and restrains evil and punishes evil. And of course 'good and evil' is here understood in the light of God's character and word.

Whenever our government is not in line with God's divine calling, we have the right to pray for and work for its removal and its replacement with a better one. But as I said earlier: the fact that we as the Church have failed to such a great degree to take responsibility for our nations in prayer, is most probably the main reason why we have the government we deserve, and not the one we need!

Why is it so important to pray for the government? First of all for the sake of the people who are under its rule. Any government has significant influence on the way its people are living, and God's heart is for the people. He wants peace, prosperity and righteousness for the people. The way the government works will either strongly encourage these goals or hinder them. This is why we need to pray for good, compassionate and righteous people in our government, who have a heart for the needs of the people.

But there is another important reason why the Church must take responsibility for our government in both prayer and action. There is no earthly government that is not ruled and influenced by the unseen powers. As a matter of fact, the government of flesh and blood is not the real ruling force. It is the unseen spiritual powers who are the real rulers of the nations and we as God's people should not forget that our struggle is, in fact, not against flesh and blood, but against the principalities and powers in the heavenlies. Any government is either under the influence of the powers of darkness or the power of the Holy Spirit. It is the Church that makes the difference. If we are a mature people who are taking our spiritual responsibility for the government seriously, then we can cut off the influence of evil occult powers on the leaders of our nation. But if we are slack and slow and uninterested in the way things are going in our country, we might see a horrible flood of evil and unrighteousness coming upon our people through a corrupt government.

Principalities and Powers

This may come as a shock to some, but even the principalities and powers were created by God (Colossians 1:16). That being so makes the Church responsible for whatever these evil powers are up to.

Remember that we have a struggle against principalities and powers. Also, remember that through the cross we have been raised up with Christ and seated with Him in heavenly places high above principalities and powers, and every name

28

that can be named in heaven and upon earth; yes, even below the earth (Ephesians 1:20–21 and 2:6).

As such, the Church has not only a responsibility to deal with the powers of darkness, but also the power and authority to do so. Anyway, who else is there who can keep a check on what these powers are doing? Only those who have come alive spiritually and have access to the unseen realm, have the possibility of confronting demonic beings. Since we shall be dealing more in depth with this subject later on when we consider 'spiritual warfare', it is sufficient here to establish that the Church is responsible for the activities of the spiritual powers.

Israel

God created the nations and, among them, one in particular. The nation of Israel. The biblical evidence to this fact is overwhelming. The election of Israel as God's people is actually a major focus in the whole of the Old Testament, and although the nation of Israel was put aside because of disobedience, it was not for ever; only for a time in history.

Romans 9–11 confirms that God never rejected the Jewish people, but planned to restore them and bring them back in to their original calling. This being so means that we as the Church are responsible for co-working with God, because all that God created has become an area for our interest and concern. The reason why we should love the Jewish people and work for their full restoration is none other than the fact that God cares for them and wants them restored.

Acts 15:16–18 declares that the rebuilding of the fallen *'tabernacle of David'* will serve the purpose of bringing the good news to the nations who have not yet heard. There is no doubt in my mind that the restoration of the nation of Israel to their ancient land is linked to God's overall plan for the nations, and with His plan of bringing forth the kingdom of God upon the earth.

In Acts 3:21 it is mentioned that heaven will hold back the Lord Jesus until the times of restoration, when all things will be restored, *'which God has spoken by the mouth of all His holy prophets since the world began'*. What did the prophets of old speak of? Among many things that they prophesied is that at the end of this age, God would bring back to the promised land all the Jewish people from the four corners of the earth to which He dispersed them, and restore them as a nation. And in the end, He would pour out His Holy Spirit upon them and then they would recognize their true Messiah, the Lord Jesus. This was foretold by the prophets Isaiah, Jeremiah, Ezekiel, Zechariah and others, and the Scripture references are so numerous that it should not be necessary to list them.

However, if the restoration of Israel is interlinked with the coming back of the Lord Jesus, then this issue must be one of highest priority for the Church.

And yet, we see today that the majority of believers in the Church are either indifferent to this matter or even against it. Many have been wrongly taught that those sections of God's word speaking about a restoration of physical Israel are not meant to be taken literally, but should be spiritual-ized as referring to the Church. But the people who advocate such a view are themselves confused. How can it be that they, at the same time, have no problem believing in a literal meaning and fulfillment of the Old Testament Scriptures about the Messiah?

Didn't the prophet Micah, for example, prophesy that Jesus the Messiah would be born in a certain physical loca-tion, namely the village of Bethlehem (Micah 5:2)? This word was spoken 500 years before it actually happened and nobody in the Christian world has any problem in accepting that as a physical reality. But when the prophets state that in the last days God will bring back the scattered people of Israel to their ancient homeland, then all of a sudden this must not be taken literally. Instead, it is interpreted as being symbolic, talking about bringing the people of the Church into unity in Christ. Strange – and, I dare say, a bit foolish! All the more so, because we have the physical evidence today right before our very eyes. God is actually fulfilling the words of His prophet in a literal sense. The newspapers have written about it almost daily for the last couple of years. Since the downfall of communism, about 1.5 million Russian Jews have already returned to Israel.

Chapter 4

If My People

'If My people who are called by My name will humble themselves, and pray and seek My face, and turn from their wicked ways, then I will hear from heaven, and will forgive their sin and heal their land.'

(2 Chronicles 7:14)

It should be clear from this Scripture how crucial the Church's role is for the destiny of the nations. God promises here that He will bring healing to the land, if His people will fulfill their calling and play their role. It is an amazing thought that there is a possibility for our nations to experience the healing power of God, and how we need that power among the nations today.

God promises that He will bless and touch a country whenever His people, the Church, are willing to fulfill His conditions. This might be a new perspective to some, but actually there is more than one biblical precedence for such a thing.

Just think about God's promises to Abraham; that He would spare the twin-cities of Sodom and Gomorrah if 10 righteous people could be found in them. For the sake of 10 righteous, God was willing to spare the lives of 10,000 people! That certainly is a testimony to the great compassionate heart of God. No-one should ever think that God is a strict and stingy God who requires a lot before He pardons people. For He is a tender and merciful God, whose strongest element of character is grace and mercy. Unfortunately, this minimum of God's requirement could not be met in Sodom and Gomorrah. We would normally say that the people in these cities perished because of the excess of their sins. But there is also another way of looking at it: the people actually perished in the flames of God's judgment, because of a lack of righteous people. This is how important and crucial the Church's position is in the city and in the nation.

In the case of Nineveh, there was a much better result. You will remember how God called His servant Jonah to go and warn the citizens of Nineveh about their rebellion and sins. But he was not willing, being caught up in his narrow religious beliefs and his natural contempt towards the heathen peoples. However, God took the trouble to make him willing, and, in the end, he went to Nineveh and delivered the message that brought about real repentance and the salvation of 120,000 people who were doomed to perdition.

The role of Jonah in relation to Nineveh is the role of the Church in relation to the cities and nations of this world. God has no servant or instrument in the world today other than His Church and, true to say, we have often been like Jonah unwilling to go, because we are caught up in religious prejudice and egoism and, consequently, the peoples of this world are facing God's judgment.

In the parable of the potter and the clay recorded in Jeremiah 18, God says that He is dealing with nations according to their way of responding to His word. If a nation can be turned to observe God's fundamental requirements it will be built and restored and blessed. But if it disregards His commandments it will be plucked up, removed and destroyed. God is dealing with nations, and His people, the Church, hold the key to the future destiny of the nations. Will it be judgment and extermination? Or will it be healing and revival? The Church will make the difference.

If my people will . . .

Humble Themselves

God has set up four requirements for His people to fulfill before He can come and heal the land.

It is important for us to observe that there are four, not one! We very often tend to be too one-sided. I suppose this is the reason behind all our tragic divisions. We get so hooked on one thing, that we lose our balance and become extreme.

Lutherans become so taken up with grace that they forget there is also something called good works. Baptists major so much on the correct form of water-baptism that they tend to forget that conversion and new birth is far more important than the outward form. For Pentecostals, the fire of the Spirit is the big thing, but often tongues, signs and wonders overshadow the importance of grace and the fruit of the Spirit in the inner life. Charismatics, of course, have had a number of over-emphasized and distorted truths like faith, discipleship, inner healing, Israel etc. Also, in the area of ministry in which I am involved we have suffered from a distortion in the realm of prayer and, particularly, spiritual warfare. As long as we just practised prayer and went after the demons, we didn't need to be concerned with anything else. If someone had asked me years ago what I thought was the one thing needed to turn the nation around, I would not have hesitated but answered prayer and only prayer! I simply believed in prayer. Today I believe in God, and prayer is only one of the things needed.

God requires four things, and the first one is: humble yourselves! And how important this is. Because what would it profit if we prayed and prayed and prayed, if God did not listen to us? Is not the whole idea of prayer that God will listen and answer? And unless we know how to humble ourselves before God we can forget about being heard in heaven.

You remember the parable Jesus spoke about the Pharisee and the tax collector. They were both standing in the temple offering up their prayers. The Pharisee prayed and said:

> *'"God, I thank you that I am not like other men – extortioners, unjust, adulterers, or even as this tax collector. I fast twice a week; I give tithes of all that I possess." And the tax collector, standing afar off, would not so much as raise his eyes to heaven, but beat his breast, saying, "God, be merciful to me a sinner!"'*   (Luke 18:11–13)

What was the Lord's response? Jesus said:

> *'"I tell you, this man* (the tax collector) *went down to his house justified rather than the other; for everyone who exalts himself will be abased, and he who humbles himself will be exalted."'*   (Luke 18:14)

In other words: the Lord did not listen to the Pharisee. All his boasting and self-righteous prayers were totally ignored by God, because his heart was full of pride. But the tax collector, who humbled himself before God, went home justified!

If there is anything God despises it is pride. Actually, pride is the gravest of all sins. This is not the way we look at it, but it is the way God looks at it. To us, the grave sins are various types of immorality, and when someone in the Church commits such they are always condemned and punished severely. But we don't seem to mind proud people so much. Pastors and spiritual leaders in the Church can be full of pride and arrogance and nobody – or only few – seem to mind, and many are actually applauding such 'great men'. But they are actually the big sinners, who should be corrected and, if unrepentant, thrown out of the Church, because pride is the root of all evil, and pride causes God to stir up much anger.

Isn't that what the Scripture says?

> *'God resists the proud, but gives grace to the humble.'*
>
> (1 Peter 5:5)

If, therefore, we have pride in our hearts, we have turned

God into our enemy and He will be resisting us all the way. How awesome a thing this is! We have our hands full having to battle against the devil and keep up with his evil schemes. Having God as our opponent means the end of everything. That would finish us all off in no time. But if we are willing to humble ourselves, we open ourselves up for a flow of grace, and God will hear our plea and respond to our prayers.

In the Church to-day, there are different suggestions as to what might be our greatest need in this hour. Some claim that it is faith. Others say that we need more anointing. My humble contribution after twenty-five years 'on the road' in full-time ministry, travelling throughout the world and visiting all parts of the Body of Christ is this: the greatest need in the world-wide Church of Jesus Christ at this time is humility!

For without learning to humble ourselves and to live in humility we shall never be able to lay hold of the grace of God. And without that, nothing, absolutely nothing else matters.

Pray

Of course, we would have anticipated that prayer would be one of the requirements for revival and the healing of our land. At least, we ought to have understood that from our knowledge of the history of the Church. There has never been a national revival anywhere in the world at any time in history that was not generated through prayer, and I mean real prayer: massive, united and persevering prayer by a hungry and desperate Church!

Also, there is no other way to revival according to the biblical testimony. We can forget, once and for all, about all these modern charismatic ideas for bringing revival; like commanding the Holy Spirit to be poured out; or starting a spiritual filibuster of worship; or using excessive spiritual warfare. All this is what I call charismatic tricks or hocus pocus and it serves only to take away our attention from the real thing, and causes us to waste our time.

The New Testament is abundantly clear: the Holy Spirit is poured out as a result of united, persevering prayer by the Church! Reading the book of Acts will confirm this.

But it is not just prayer in any way. There is a lot of misconception about prayer. Often it has developed into religion. Prayer is being used wrongly to fulfill selfish ambitions or to exhibit people's spirituality. Thus, prayer can turn into story-telling or a presentation of Bible studies.

To pray simply means to make requests! This is something we need to come back to in the Church today. We need to learn to dare to give God specific requests. To ask Him to do the great things we need in our nation. Because He is a great God, worthy of great petitions and well able to give us exceedingly far above what we ask or even think! The funny thing is that God's people do not ask for much. Our prayers have sunk down to the level of what is humanly possible, and if all we dare believe for is humanly possible, we hardly need God.

The Father challenges His Son in Psalm 2 by saying:

> *'Ask of Me, and I will give You the nations for Your inheritance, and the ends of the earth for Your posses-sion.'* (Psalm 2:8)

It is time for us to make concrete requests to God for our nation. Like the Scottish reformer, John Knox, who came before God in a time of great need for Scotland and prayed: 'Lord, give me Scotland or I die!' God honored this faithful man of prayer and gave him Scotland through sending over the land what is known as the Presbyterian revival.

Seek His Face

If you will seek My face, I will heal your land.

This is more than just praying. Seeking God's face goes deeper. It means that we actually come face to face with the Lord. God wants us to get away from praying our own thing, and come to the point where we can be fully available for the burdens of the Holy Spirit.

Prayer is not so much taking our concerns to the Lord as it is learning to listen to what is upon His heart. It is the experience of many that we can be seeking God for a long time and wonder why we never find Him. The reason is that we seek Him according to our mindset and tradition instead of seeking Him according to His way.

For many years, in my Pentecostal upbringing, I used to wonder why I could spend so much time in prayer and never seem to get in touch with the Lord. Later, I realized that the problem was not with the Lord, but with me. I was seeking Him 'the Pentecostal way' by insisting that He should reveal Himself according to my expectations. But if we are not willing to put down our own thoughts and ways we are not really seeking God's face.

Many years ago, I met a sister who had been seeking God for the baptism of the Spirit for a total of 11 years. And to no avail. Then she came to me to ask why God had not responded to her prayers. I asked her what she had been expecting to receive from God when she had been praying for this experience. To which she answered that she would absolutely not have it like 'these Pentecostals'. In other words, she had been seeking God according to her own understanding and desires and not coming before Him with empty hands, ready to receive His gifts according to His way. That was the simple reason why she had been seeking God for 11 years without any answer.

> '*Seek the Lord while He may be found, Call upon Him while He is near. Let the wicked forsake his way, And the unrighteous man his thoughts; Let him return to the* LORD *... For My thoughts are not your thoughts, Nor are your ways My ways ... For as the heavens are higher than the earth, So are My ways higher than your ways, And my thoughts than your thoughts.*' (Isaiah 55:6–9)

Wickedness and unrighteousness are not all that constitute

grave sin. It is simply anything that deviates from God's will and way. Going our own way and doing our own thing is evil in the sight of God, and clinging on to our own thoughts in seeking God will most certainly mean that we are going to miss the Lord. We must learn to lay down all our own self and come before God with empty hands ready to hear His voice and do His will. That is what it means to seek God's face, and that kind of consecration and availability is a requirement if we are going to see God heal our land.

Turn Away From Your Wicked Ways

This is the fourth requirement. It speaks about repentance. God requires true repentance as a prerequisite for the healing of the land. It is my experience, that we believers do not fully understand what repentance is. We often confuse it with forgiveness, but asking for forgiveness and receiving it, is not the same as repentance.

Repentance requires more than that. It requires that we change our way radically and stop doing the same thing anymore. That is the real meaning of the word repent: to change your direction! To confess a sin, ask for forgiveness and receive it, is something we can do over and over again, but that does not mean that we have repented of it. Unless we change direction completely and turn our backs on our wicked ways, we have not repented in the true, biblical sense of that word.

A couple of years ago, the Lord taught me a lesson of repentance. I was travelling through Heathrow airport in London and standing in line to get through customs. Behind me was an British gentleman and his friend pushing a cart with their luggage. All of a sudden, he pushed his cart into my heels. I turned around and when the gentleman discovered his 'sin', he said with a thick Oxford accent: 'I am so sorry!' I smiled and turned back.

A little later down the line, the same thing happened. Apparently, the man was so eagerly caught up in talking to his friend that he did not notice where he was driving his cart. I turned around and this time my smile was a bit stiff. He apologized again, and on we went. Then, for a third time, he drove his cart into me. I turned around and this time there was no smile on my face. I looked at the man and he quickly issued his usual apology: 'I am so sorry!' in line with the best of British traditions. I replied: 'Sir, instead of being so repeatedly sorry would you mind opening your eyes and looking where you are pushing this thing?' He blushed and quickly pulled the cart out of the line until I had disappeared completely behind the customs wall.

Well inside the passport control the Lord arrested me in my thoughts: 'Johannes, was this a good Christian response to the problem?' I had to confess I had reacted in the flesh. But then the Lord pointed this out to me: the British gentleman had asked forgiveness three times, but he had never once repented!

I came to think about how true this is. How many times in the Charismatic movement have we not asked forgiveness of one another for our denominational pride and barriers, and yet nothing much has changed. We are still hiding behind the same old walls. Once in a while we come out and celebrate, performing our love for one another on the platform as it were. Kissing and hugging all types of Christians, asking forgiveness for our sins of division. But have we truly repented and changed our ways of living, radically? The answer is no! Until we turn from our wicked ways we can not make a way for the Lord to come and heal our land.

Chapter 5

Confessing the Sins of the Nation

The reason why many believers have difficulties understanding the significance of praying for the nations can be found in the fact that they have never discovered the far reaching effects of the redemptive work of the cross. If the blood of Jesus was shed only for the believers in the Church, then there is hardly any reason to bother with anything but the affairs of the Church. Then God has no issue with nations, and is also not interested in all of creation. If this is so, then why should we ever waste any time praying for the nations or caring for the way things are going with the world?

Jesus Died for the Sins of the Whole World

However, redemption reaches far beyond the little flock of saved ones. The apostle John in his first letter says that if we sin, we have a propitiation for our sins, and not only for our sins, but for the sins of the whole world (1 John 2:1–2)!

Jesus died for more than the sins of the Church. He died for the sins of the whole world, and although that does not mean universal salvation, it does mean that provision has been made not only for individual sin, but also for national sins and historical sins.

Furthermore, the apostle Paul in his second letter to the Corinthians confirms this global effect of the cross. In 2 Corinthians 5:16–21, he points out that reconciliation is for much more than individual to individual. It is aimed at the whole world:

> *'God was in Christ reconciling the world to Himself . . . '*
> (2 Corinthians 5:19)

The world is far more than the Church. God's heart embraces all that He ever created, and He longs to be reconciled to it all. For the Lord never created anything with the purpose of destruction.

Paul follows up on this interesting subject in Romans 8:17–25. The whole of Creation, he says, is under bondage and corruption because of sin, and it cries out, eagerly waiting for the *'revealing of the sons of God'*. It is God's purpose to incorporate all of Creation into the *'glorious liberty of the children of God'*. In other words: the cross embraces all of creation. Redemption is meant to reach out and touch everything that has been created according to God's eternal purposes. The blood of Jesus covers all of Creation and is the ransom to redeem it from all the consequences of sin.

If we are 'ambassadors for Christ' advocating reconciliation between God and His creation – and if Christ has already provided atonement for the sins of the whole world, then we, the Church, must have the calling and the means of standing in the gap for the nation. We play the role as the intercessor pleading the cause of our land before God.

There is one major problem that stands in the way of the healing of the land. That is the unconfessed historical sins of the nation. Unconfessed sin is the foothold of satanic forces, whether we speak of the individual or the nation. Unconfessed sin constitutes a basis for satanic rule. We must therefore find a way of dealing with it, if we are to see our people delivered from demonic strongholds. In speaking about a nation there is a principle of solidarity with effect to sin.

According to Romans 5:12, sin came into this world through one man and it saturated into all mankind down through the generations. We are all sinners not just because of the sins we have committed, but even before we were able

to commit sin. We were born sinners because of this principle of solidarity. This is actually one of the greatest stum-
bling stones for the unbelievers, and in many ways they feel
God has treated them unfairly. However, before we get too
busy blaming God for this unfortunate fact, we ought to be
reminded of another fact: God has already provided the
solution to this problem through the redemption of His Son,
the Lord Jesus. And He did that long before any of us were
born sinners. So, there is really no excuse.

However it is important to understand this principle when
we speak about the unconfessed sins of our people. For we
could easily think, as many do, that the past sins of generations are of no concern to us. I mean, we were not around
when our forefathers committed these things, and besides we
are now saved by God's grace and going to heaven. But this
is a very irresponsible attitude.

In one of His discussions with the Pharisees, Jesus high-
lights this matter as recorded in Matthew 23:29–36. The
Pharisees, having been out to adorn the tombs and monu-
ments of the victims of their evil forefathers, are claiming
that if they had been around in the days when these crimes
were committed, they would not have participated. But Jesus
remarkably rejects their claim, because in order to cut your-
self free from your solidarity with the past it is not enough to
bring flowers to the tombs. As long as they have not
confessed the sins of their forefathers they are still responsible.

Listen to these strong words of Jesus:

> *'Therefore you are witnesses against yourselves that you
> are sons of those who murdered the prophets. Fill up,
> then, the measure of your fathers' guilt. Serpents, brood
> of vipers! How can you escape the condemnation of hell?
> Therefore, indeed, I send you prophets, wise men, and
> scribes: some of them you will kill and crucify, and some
> of them you will scourge in your synagogues and perse-
> cute from city to city, that on you may come all the right-
> eous blood shed on the earth, from the blood of righteous*

> *Abel to the blood of Zechariah, son of Berechiah, whom*
> *you murdered between the temple and the altar. Assu-*
> *redly, I say to you, all these things will come upon this*
> *generation.'* (Matthew 23:29–36)

Jesus, knowing that the Pharisees will not confess the sins of their fathers, and knowing that they will therefore continue in these sins, makes this generation responsible for the whole history of crimes.

Wasn't that the same as God told Moses, when He gave him the commandments:

> *'... For I, the LORD, your God, am a jealous God, visit-*
> *ing the iniquity of the fathers upon the children to the*
> *third and fourth generations of those who hate Me, but*
> *showing mercy to thousands, to those who love Me and*
> *keep My commandments.'* (Deuteronomy 5:9–10)

The effects and the curse of sin continue if it goes on unconfessed. That is why a way must be found to confess the unconfessed sins, so that the ban may be lifted and the people under its curse be set free. And who is going to do it? Remember we are talking about sins being committed in the past by people who are long since dead and gone. They cannot come back to life to confess, can they? Therefore their descendants must step into the gap as intercessors to make substitute confession. Notice that we are only talking about those who are dead. The principle does not apply for those sinners who are still alive. We cannot confess the sins of people who are still around and are themselves unwilling to repent. But we can pray for such and through our prayers bring them under the convicting influence of the Holy Spirit. For those, who are long gone however, and are unable to deal with the situation, we, the Church, can act as interces-sors.

There is an example of this in 2 Samuel 21:1–2. There was a famine in Israel under the rule of king David. The famine went on for three years, until finally, David began to inquire of the Lord. The Lord then revealed to him that the reason for the famine was bloodguilt resting on the house of his predecessor king Saul. Saul and his men had violated a covenant that had been made between Joshua and the Gibeonites. The Gibeonites were not of the house of Israel, but during the capture of the promised land, facing extermination along with the other tribes in Canaan, they managed to fool Joshua and he made a covenant with them that they should be allowed to stay in the land and serve the people of Israel. Some of Saul's men in a situation of conflict had disregarded this covenant and killed some of the Gibeonites. Because of this violation that had not been confessed or repented of, the land came under the curse of a famine. Not until this bloodguilt had been repented of and compensation paid to the Gibeonites, was the curse lifted, and rain began to fall again in Israel after three years.

David had to make the confession. But he had had no part in this whole story. Actually, he could claim that Saul, the former king, had turned against him and persecuted him. But unfortunately, Saul had been dead for some time, and it could not be expected that he would be ressurrected from his grave to bring this matter in order. So David, the new king, had to take responsibility and on behalf of the past generation provide atonement for the sin committed.

Well, this role can also be seen in the life of the great intercessors of the Bible. Moses had to step into the gap, confess the sins of rebellious Israel and save them from being destroyed by the wrath of God. Daniel also became the intercessor for the Jewish people in captivity in Babylon. He discovered one day as he was reading the book of Jeremiah that the time for the 70 years of the Babylonian captivity was coming to an end. He then humbled himself before God and began confessing the sins of his people; the sins that had led to their captivity.

Once again, Daniel had not personally been involved in the sins of his forefathers, but they were no longer around, and he felt the call to take their place before God and confess their sins as his own sins. Actually, it was this action by Daniel that opened up the way for the return of the Jewish people from Babylon to Israel.

Let me close this subject by bringing a concrete example of the power and blessing that follows when the Church confesses the sins of the nation.

When I started to minister in Germany in 1980, helping to pioneer Intercessors for Germany, I was still living in Copenhagen, Denmark, with my family. They were not easy days. Every time I crossed the border between Denmark and Germany and entered German soil I felt a strong depressive power coming against me. It was as if the German nation was lying under a big dark cloud. I soon realized that this spiritual oppression was almost a natural consequence of the guilt for the holocaust against the Jewish people under the Nazi time and Germany's war crimes as a whole in this century.

At that time, there was the beginning of a movement of repentance for this among the German believers, spearheaded by the evangelical sisterhood of Mary in Darmstadt. Actually, this group of very committed and consecrated sisters had started their pleading with God for forgiveness and mercy not long after the end of the war. But apart from them, there was little understanding of the subject among the evangelical churches. As the German prayer-movement started to grow under the leadership of Berthold Becker, this issue became more and more pressing, and in co-operation with other leaders, a national Christian manifestation of repentance and reconciliation was planned.

This was to take place on the day of the 50th anniversary of Hitler's announcement on the 15th September 1935 of the so-called Nürnberg-laws, the beginning of the persecution of the Jewish citizens in Germany. The manifestation should then take place on the 15th September 1985 at the very same location: the giant stadium in Nürnberg, which Hitler had built for his great celebrations and the worship of himself as the Führer of Germany. It turned out to be a historical day and very moving. Around 10,000 believers from all over Germany and representing almost every part of the Body of

Christ in the nation, led by a cross-section of the spiritual leadership, came to Nürnberg.

We knelt down in the stadium in humility and tears and confessed all the evil that had started that very same day, 50 years ago. Confessions were read in unison to God and into the spiritual realm over Germany, and afterwards, we went on a silent march of mourning through the streets of Nürnberg. The whole event was filmed by the two major nation-wide television stations.

The outcome of this gathering, I know, cannot be measured in a physical way. But it is clear to me that a change took place in the spiritual atmosphere over Germany. From that day on, the growth of the German prayer-movement gained momentum, and today we have one of the strongest prayer-movements in the world here in Germany. But after that, there was also a breakthrough in evangelism and Church renewal and many new churches began to be founded.

Today as I personally live in Germany I can testify to the fact that the heavy cloud of condemnation and depression has lifted. One can also see from the miracle of the German reunification that happened in 1990, that God's blessing has returned upon the nation. We are not through yet in any way, but an important step forward was made when the Church took its responsibility seriously, and stood in the gap to confess the sins of the nation.

Chapter 6

An Awesome Army With Banners

In one of the previous chapters we made clear that it is part of the responsibility of the mature Church to face up to the activities of the powers of darkness. We are called to manifest the manifold wisdom of God to the principalities and powers in the heavenlies, that is to implement the victory of the cross of Jesus Christ upon the works of the devil. Remember that upon the cross He

> '...disarmed principalities and powers, He made a public spectacle of them, triumphing over them in it.'
>
> (Colossians 2:15)

What the Head of the Church so wonderfully accomplished must be manifested through His body, the Church.

When Jesus first began to speak to His disciples about the Church that would come out of His death and resurrection, He gave a remarkable perspective as shown in these words to Simon Peter:

> 'And I also say to you that you are Peter, and on this rock I will build My church, and the gates of Hades shall not prevail against it. And I will give you the keys of the kingdom of heaven, and whatever you bind on earth will be bound in heaven, and whatever you loose on earth will be loosed in heaven.'
>
> (Matthew 16:18–19)

There are some vital lessons here for us to learn concerning the role of the Church. Jesus is speaking about building His Church and putting it up against the gates of Hades. These are some of the first words the Lord spoke about the Church even before He had called it forth into existence. The Church was not to first and foremost confront people, but the demonic powers. Actually, we learn from this that the primary calling of the Church is not to evangelism or social work, but to spiritual warfare. The Church is not a human organisation; it is a spiritual structure with the calling and the means to oppose and overcome spiritual powers as its first priority. Then follows a work to be done in terms of evangelizing the world. To claim that spiritual warfare is not valid is to take away from the Church its principal calling and reduce it to a mere human organisation.

Jesus also pointed out in another section of Scripture that in order to touch people's lives and take them out from the power of the evil one, we must first learn to bind the strong man. And His question was this:

> '... how can one enter a strong man's house and plunder his goods, unless he first binds the strong man? And then he will plunder his house.' (Matthew 12:29)

Jesus also said that the 'casting out of demons by the Spirit of God' is the proof that the Kingdom of God is manifested among us (Matthew 12:28). Hence, if the Church rejects spiritual warfare it cannot manifest the Kingdom of God upon the earth.

Spiritual warfare and evangelism go hand in hand. Evangelism is not successful without spiritual warfare, and spiritual warfare is senseless unless it is linked to evangelism and the planting of churches. The keys of the Kingdom to bind and to loose are given in order to enable us to plunder the strong man's possessions; to set people free from demonic bondages so that they can respond to the Gospel and get saved.

Where there is revival today in our world, this principle

has been understood and practised. For instance, in Argentina, one of the pillars of the present revival is prayer-evangelism! When the Argentinian revivalists are campaigning they, first of all, send in teams of intercessors and prayer-warriors to battle against the demonic forces. Only when they have secured a break-through in the heavenlies, do they then send in the evangelists to preach the Gospel. For when the demonic yoke over people is broken, they are able to respond and hear the word of God. One very successful Argentinian evangelist is in the habit of always travelling with a team of prayer warriors. He has a huge tent with a portable platform. Under his platform is a prayer room where some 25 intercessors are praying and doing spiritual battle during the preaching of the word. When the evangelist senses that the enemy is opposing his preaching, he knocks on the floor with his foot to signal to his intercessors below that they need to increase the pressure on the demonic forces. This brother has big gospel meetings all year round in Argentina, assembling around 30,000 people every night. He is said to be the most successful city-evangelist since the days of the early Church.

We only have to look to South Korea to see this truth confirmed. South Korea has had a revival going on ever since the beginning of this century, which only stopped during the five years of Japanese occupation. This revival has been born and maintained through massive prayer and spiritual warfare by the South Korean Church. Some 30% of the population today are born again, and if the revival continues with the same power as today, it is estimated that 60% of the South Korean population will be Christians by the year 2000. One of the leading revivalists in the country, Pastor Yonggi Cho, who leads the world's biggest local church (some 700,000 members) was once asked what he thought was the secret of the South Korean revival. His answer was this: 'Very simply: we have broken through the lid of demonic forces over the land, and through our massive ongoing prayer and spiritual warfare we are maintaining the hole through the heavenlies to secure the ongoing flow of God's blessing upon our people!'

An American officer, a believer with a heart on fire for the Lord, was stationed by the US forces in Germany until he was transferred to the US forces in South Korea. While in Germany, he shared zealously with many people about the Lord but was disappointed with the poor response he met. When he came to South Korea, he continued witnessing to people, but was completely overwhelmed by the strong response. Nearly everybody he talked to about the Lord wanted to get saved, and he had to cut back on his evangelistic endeavors in the end because new converts give you a lot of work. He was so surprised with this difference in spiritual atmosphere between Germany and Korea, that he approached Yonggi Cho to get an explanation. 'I am the same here as I was in Germany, and I am doing exactly the same. Why is there such a vast difference in the reponse from the people?' Brother Cho's answer was very simple: 'Out here we have broken through in the spiritual realm and made a way through spiritual warfare for the Holy Spirit to reach down. In Germany the lid of spiritual demonic oppression is still unbroken!'

The Building of the Church

Jesus said that He would build His Church, and that it was the Church that would have the power to overcome the gates of Hades. This promise was, in other words, not given to any individual. Spiritual authority to resist principalities and powers rests with the Church. The individual believer cannot claim such power. Otherwise, there would have been no reason why the Lord wanted to build the Church. When individual Christians claim that they have the authority to go against high-level principalities they are treading on thin and dangerous ground. Basically, they take Scriptures unto themselves which were given to the Church. We, generally, suffer from a failure to see and understand the revelation of the Church, and thus have 'individualized' the New Testament.

The New Covenant is quite different from the Old in the sense that in the Old Covenant God based His work on individuals, now under the New Covenant He has based His work on the corporate being of His Church. Consequently, the New Testament speaks in a corporate sense. When Paul speaks about the battle against principalities and powers in his letter to the Ephesians, he uses the word 'we', not 'I', and his whole letter is **about** the Body of Christ, the Church, and **to** the Body of Christ. The letter is not addressed to individuals but to the assembly of saints in Ephesus. Thus, spiritual warfare becomes a matter for the Church. How much we need to commit ourselves to building up the Church into unity and maturity so that we might have the power and authority to overcome the gates of Hades.

One can hear the heartcry of the Apostle, when, in Ephesians 4, he is pleading for the building up of the body in love and unity:

> *'... till we all come to the unity of the faith and the knowledge of the Son of God, to a perfect man, to the measure of the stature of the fullness of Christ; that we should no longer be children, tossed to and fro and carried about with every wind of doctrine, by the trickery of men, in the cunning craftiness by which they lie in wait to deceive, but, speaking the truth in love, may grow up in all things into Him who is the head – Christ.'*
>
> (Ephesians 4:13–15)

We see from this that the discernment and power to overcome the deceiving forces and schemes of the devil lies in the building of the Church. This fact is, of course, no secret to the devil. Therefore, his strategy from the beginning has been to destroy the true testimony of the Church. As long as he can keep the Body of Christ divided, he can keep his dominion over places and people intact. That is why we need to understand that it is not enough to have church-planting and church growth only in the numeric sense. We need the quality of unity and love in the building up of the

Church. For by Church we do not mean the institution of the denomination; we mean the one and only Body of Christ consisting of all the living stones in a given locality. God has only one Church in every place, and that is the Church we need to join the Lord in building. It seems to be 'in' today to have as big a church as possible, and of course as many as possible. I am all for it, but I would like to point out that God wants church growth in more than just the numerical sense. He wants His Church to grow up into spiritual manhood, into the fullness of Christ, so that, as in the early days, we can speak of the believers having *'one heart and one soul'*, being of *'one accord'*, being in such agreement with one another that they could ask anything and were able to bind and loose as promised in Matthew 18:18–20.

The well-known charismatic pastor, Juan Carlos from Argentina, learned a valuable lesson from the Lord in this area. Many years ago, he arrived at a new place in Argentina to pastor a small church of about 50 members. Juan, being a fiery evangelist, managed to see his new church grow to around 200 people in only one year, after which it seemed to explode and grow to 600 in the course of only another few years. Then there came a point when brother Juan became very exhausted and went away into the mountains to seek the Lord in prayer and fasting. He cried out of his heart to the Lord and said: 'Lord, you see how my little church has been growing and growing, and now the work is so demanding that I do not know what to do!' The Lord very gently answered his servant: 'Juan, your church has not been growing at all!' Juan was shocked with this statement, and so he immediately said to the Lord: 'But Lord, in one year we grew from 50 to 200 and over the last couple of years we have grown to more than 600' 'Your church has not been growing,' the Lord insisted, 'three years ago you were 50 lukewarm Christians, and now you are 600 lukewarm Christians. What's the difference? Your church has not grown, it has only become fat!'

It was this experience which led Juan Carlos to understand the need of discipling the believers and also to divide the church congregation into what is now known as cell-groups. He realised that God is never satisfied with mere numbers. He wants His children to grow-up into spiritual maturity. He is also not satisfied with many big churches. He wants a Church strong in love and unity and living in the fullness of Christ. Only the building of such a Church can threaten the gates of Hell.

What are these gates of Hell? The word 'hell' is used by the Old King James version, and we must assume that it refers to the satanic powers. 'Gates' is a word brought up from the Old Testament. The 'gates' means the seat of government. In the cities of Israel, it was customary that the elders of the city would sit and rule in the gates. We, as God's Church, are up against satanic strongholds in the air over our cities and nations, counsels of darkness conspiring to destroy the Church and the peoples of our society. God has His answer: the super-structure of His people, the Church, who being built according to the design of Jesus will have the power to overthrow these strongholds and destroy their evil counsel.

Chapter 7

The Art of Prayer Warfare

We have seen that spiritual warfare is essential for the Church if she is to be that 'powerhouse of God' that He designed her to be. It is therefore vital that we come to a true understanding of this whole subject. Today, there is a lot of confusion as to what can be done and what cannot be done through spiritual warfare, and the excesses go all the way from some people completely rejecting the whole thing to those who seem to believe that spiritual warfare will solve everything. In the midst of much fantasy and imagination in this area, there is a dire need to consider some biblical substance for what we are doing and develop a 'theology' of spiritual warfare.

A Word of Definition

The phrase 'spiritual warfare' cannot be found in the Scriptures. Therefore, some people say that it is a term that we, in the Church, have adopted from the occult movements. It is a fact that 'spiritual warfare' has been practised for decades among occult people. For them, it means to come together and issue curses against people and, in particular, against Christians and their leaders. But, we do not want to 'borrow' anything from the occult movement, and, our spiritual warfare certainly does not have anything to do with hocus-pocus against anything. We are also not communicating directly with the powers of darkness. Biblical spiritual warfare is something quite different. It is the art of prayer, and prayer means communicating with God, not with Satan. For this reason, I find it much better and safer if we talk about 'prayer warfare' instead of 'spiritual warfare'. That it is a type of prayer according to the Bible is beyond any doubt.

When Jesus spoke in Matthew 18 about binding and loosing, He explained it clearly in the context of agreeing in prayer. When Paul is talking about our struggle in Ephesians 6, he, first of all, makes it clear that we can never fight against flesh or blood; against human beings. It is strictly forbidden to use spiritual weapons against any person, not even against anyone whom we might consider our worst enemy, or the worst enemy of the Gospel or the Church. Even our worst enemies of flesh and blood are human beings whom God loves, and we are told to love our enemies and bless those who are persecuting us. No, our battle is against the real enemies of mankind and the Church, the demonic powers of evil in the heavenlies.

Furthermore, Paul explains this battle against the powers in the context of being in the mode or attitude of prayer. His conclusion of the whole portion of Scriptures in Ephesians 6, where he teaches about this subject, is that we should do this *'always praying in the Spirit'*. In other words, spiritual warfare is prayer; it is born in prayer, led in prayer and exercised through prayer. Without prayer, it does not exist. For that reason, nobody should think for a moment that spiritual warfare can substitute for the discipline of ordinary prayer. If we have not learned to give ourselves to prayer and intercession we will never be able to touch the realities of spiritual warfare.

The great benefit of seeing this as prayer warfare is that it teaches us that our confrontation with the powers of darkness always goes via the throne of God, and never directly. Whenever we are coming against the enemy we are coming through the Lord, led by His Holy Spirit, since we are told to do this always praying in the Spirit. Previously, in the same chapter of Ephesians, we are told to *'be strong in the Lord and in the power of His might'* (Ephesians 6:10), because if we are not encountering the enemy from the position of being 'in Christ', led by His Word and His Spirit, we will get nowhere in the battle, and we will most certainly find ourselves in deep trouble. When Paul in 2 Corinthians 10:4 speaks about our spiritual weapons of warfare, he says that they are *'mighty in God for pulling down strongholds'*. It is through God – through Him alone – that we are able to confront and overcome the evil powers.

By the term 'praying in the Spirit', Paul does not mean 'speaking in tongues' as some would have it. There are people in prayer ministry who are teaching that 'praying in the Spirit' always equals praying in tongues, and that praying in tongues is a very strong weapon we have against Satan. Both these conceptions are not scripturally correct and are causing a lot of trouble to people who engage themselves in the spiritual battle.

First of all 'praying in the Spirit' with a capital 'S' is not equal to praying in tongues, whereas 'praying in the spirit' with a small 's' is. Paul in 1 Corinthians 14 goes to a great length explaining this matter and uses the whole chapter to do so. He speaks about *'praying with the mind'* and *'praying with the spirit'*, meaning, of course, that in prayer I can use my normal language or I can use the gift of tongues. He evaluates the use of the mind over the use of tongues for the sake of the assembly in prayer as well as in singing because when we are together in the fellowship of the Church it is important that we can understand one another in order to be one in prayer. But, of course, doing it all 'in the Spirit' meaning the Holy Spirit, is another matter.

We need to understand that God wants us to pray both with our minds in the Spirit as well as pray with our spirits 'in the Spirit'. It is possible to do both these things 'out of the Spirit' as it were, as well as, for that matter, so many other things that we are able to do without necessarily being in the Holy Spirit. If I have received the gift of tongues I can speak in tongues anytime I like, but that does not mean that I am always doing it in the Spirit. In the same way I can speak words of prayer with my mind, but that does not mean that I am necessarily uttering them in the Holy Spirit.

To claim then that praying in tongues is equal to praying in the Holy Spirit is completely wrong! And again, unfortunately, this false teaching has led to a lot of confusion and disappointment among praying people. While in Central America some years ago, I heard during a large prayer rally how one of the leading prayer leaders advised a sister who had had trouble knowing how to pray for her nation, to just close her eyes and pray in tongues for an hour. Problem solved. This is the one of the most absurd things I have ever heard! We should teach people to intercede in an intelligent way as they pray for their country and not give them this kind of rubbish. Paul's teaching on tongues makes it very clear that whoever speaks in tongues does not understand what he says, but is communicating secretly with God. How does that work then when we need to ask God for specific things according to His revealed will? For that is the clear prerequisite for having our prayers heard and answered!

Furthermore, the gift of tongues is not a weapon to be used in prayer warfare. There has been some talk among some Charismatics of 'war-tongues', which is pure fantasy. Besides, the use of speaking in tongues against Satan is an abuse of one of the most wonderful gifts of the Spirit. Again 1 Corinthians 14 puts things in the right perspective for us. According to Paul's teaching here, the gift of speaking in tongues is for personal edification. It is for communication between our spirit and God's Spirit so that we might open up for the work of the Spirit. The wonderful effect of this gift is to bring us in touch with the Holy Spirit; bring us into God's presence, so that we can hear from God and receive His word and His direction. Nowhere in the New Testament are we told to use speaking in tongues to scare the devil away. This idea comes from naive and immature people, who don't know what they are saying. No, speaking in tongues is for personal edification to build up our spirit, to touch the Lord and enter into His throne-room.

It is through such unbiblical practices that the whole issue of spiritual warfare is being discredited and misrepresented in the eyes of many sincere believers, who have a desire to honor the written Word of God. And it is a great pity because it also means that parts of the Body of Christ through encountering these false teachings are throwing the baby out with the bath water. Let us try to find sound and valid biblical grounds for all our doings, and not be swayed by our own imaginations.

To Know Our Mission

We must try to find out what can be done through prayer warfare, and also what cannot be done. Also, we need to know our mission in prayer warfare. Obviously, without such knowledge we could easily engage ourselves in wasting a lot of time on issues that are not valid. And our enemy is eager to try to deceive us into activities that are imaginary and will only serve to wear us out in the battle.

Already we have experienced the most strange and bizarre attempts by believers to unsettle the enemy. I have personally been present when intercessors in their zeal for the Lord have attacked the devil and strangled him, or stabbed him in the back with a big knife, or sent him hungering and thirsting out into the Sahara desert. Others have put a millstone around his neck in an act of spiritual warfare and sunk him down into the deepest spot in the Pacific Ocean. Others again have developed a habit of driving great principalities around in the world from continent to continent, just as if that in itself would solve any problems. Instead it would mean that we transfer our problems to our brothers and sisters abroad.

Once in America, I watched a Christian television programme. The preacher, a well known tele-evangelist, was teaching his audience to treat the devil like you treat an undisciplined dog. 'Sit!' 'Stand!' 'Run!' 'Shut up!' This poor fellow obviously had never read the letter of the apostle Jude, who warns us against such foolishness. How much must we tolerate of self-fabricated nonsense before some-body blows the whistle?

The idea of killing the devil suits me well, and I wish it could be done. But the word of God clearly tells us that God Himself has given the devil a certain space and a certain time in history, and until that has been fulfilled we will have to get used to the idea of having him around. God has appointed a day, according to the book of Revelation, where He will deal with Satan, binding him first for a thousand years, and then casting him into the lake of fire with all his principalities and powers. Until that glorious day dawns there is no way we can get rid of them for good. Therefore, instead of wasting our time and energy in trying to do what cannot be done, we should rather concentrate on that which we can do, and then leave the rest to the Lord.

According to the word of God, there are basically three things the Church can do to the principalities and powers of darkness. We can silence them; we can bind them and we can pull down their strongholds. That, to me, seems to be good enough, and if we could only learn to practise that we would be able to accomplish much in the spiritual battle. These three functions are the role of the Church acting in its corporate authority, and are different from the individual authority to cast out demons, which believers also have in the name of Jesus.

It is Psalm 8 which tells us about the possibility of silencing the adversary:

> '*Out of the mouth of babes and infants You have ordained strength, because of Your enemies, that You may silence the enemy and the avenger.*'   (Psalm 8:2)

This is amazing! God is able to bring the enemy to silence, not by stirring up the power of the mighty heroes, but by a proclamation that comes out of the mouth of babies. Of course, this is just like God. His foolishness is wiser than the wisdom of men and His weakness stronger than the strength of men (1 Corinthians 1:25). When He came out against all the works of the devil, He chose a child in a manger and the death of His dear Son in much weakness to confound and completely destroy the powers of evil. In the same way, He has chosen His little flock of weak and ordinary people like you and me to shut the mouth of the accuser and leave him standing there defeated and dumbfounded!

To silence the devil is a powerful and very needy thing, because his foremost weapon is to talk to and accuse people. The primary battle in which we find ourselves is the battle for the mind. It is more or less in our thought life that the battle will be won or lost. The devil is constantly bombarding God's people by speaking into their minds. In this way, he is trying to distract us from communicating with the Lord and hearing His voice. It is, therefore, tremendously important that we become aware of our authority to silence the enemy.

This is also very important when we speak of the Church, because as we assemble together to worship the Lord and to hear His word, the enemy will become very active in trying to distract our minds and make us lose our concentration. Jesus made that clear through the parable of the sower and the seed. The seed being the word of the Lord and the soil representing our hearts. He said that when the seed fell on the ground, the birds of the air would be there to pick it up before it could get into the soil. The birds of the air symbolize the demonic powers who will always seek to prevent us from even listening when we are under the preaching of God's word. They do that by shooting thoughts into our mind so that we become absent-minded and fail to hear what is being said.

As a former church-pastor and as a preacher of God's word for many years, I have noticed this problem in standing in front of an assembly of God's people. Sometimes, you can even see in a physical way how some of the audience are distracted and carried away in their minds from being present and attentive in the meeting. They are still there in the hall in their bodies, but they are miles away in their minds. For many years, I tried to ignore the problem, excusing people as being tired or having had a hard week.

But then I became aware that the same problem would often manifest itself during times of vacation when work and tiredness, etc., were not a factor. And I began to see that the sleepiness and the lack of concentration were not of the natural category, but a very deliberate strategy from the enemy.

The Bible says in the book of Daniel chapter 7 verse 25, that the strategy of the anti-Christian spirit is *'to wear out the saints'*! It is most probably that which is meant in 1 Peter 5:8 where the devil is portrayed as a roaring lion going around and seeking whom he may devour. Devour means to preoccupy, to beset people in their minds so that they are not free to hear from God and to respond to His word. This is not a word describing the devil's work in the world among unbelievers, but a word that speaks about his activity among the saints. He is ever present at church meetings seeking to disrupt our time by confusing our minds through his endless talking. We should no longer tolerate this activity, but we should know that God has given us the authority to silence him so that the whole Church might be alert in the spirit, able to hear and receive from the Lord, able to praise and worship the Lord in freedom. Many times I have seen meetings being turned around completely because the leadership in a concrete way stood up against the interference of the powers of darkness and commanded them to be silent. Also, I have seen whole conferences 'saved' from otherwise apparent failure through using prayer warfare to shut the mouth of the adversary.

Binding the Kings

Another expression which is used to describe the nature of prayer warfare is the word 'binding'. This word occurs in both the Old and New Testament several times. One such clear statement is found in Psalm 149:5–9:

> *'Let the saints be joyful in glory; Let them sing aloud on their beds. Let the high praises of God be in their mouth,*

And a two-edged sword in their hand, To execute vengeance on the nations, And punishments on the peoples; To bind their kings with chains, And their nobles with fetters of iron; To execute on them the written judgment – This honor have all His saints. Praise the Lord!'

First of all, take notice of the great connection between joy and prayer warfare. Prayer warfare is not meant to be a heavy and depressing ministry, but something that is done with the heart full of joy and praise. This, of course, is because, as we have already seen, our focus is not on the darkness but on the throne of God where Christ sits at the right-hand side of the Father, having been given all authority in heaven and on earth. Thus, we are assured that the battle is not ours but the Lord's and that He has already secured the victory through His cross. Spiritual warfare must be a joyful ministry in the Church, otherwise we have taken a wrong spiritual approach to it.

Secondly, it sounds quite unusual that they are lying on their beds while handling a two-edged sword. But this is another reference to the fact that prayer warfare should be fought out of a position of rest in the Lord and not in the strenuous sweat of carnal efforts.

We are told here that our assignment is to bind the kings with chains. The kings mentioned here are, of course, not earthly kings of flesh and blood, but just another word for the 'princes', the principalities of the heavenlies. We have no arguments with any monarch of the nations of this world, but we do with the hierarchy of satanic world rulers. We have been authorized to bind them. That does not mean to kill them, as we said earlier. When you bind a person you do not take his life, but you paralyze him and make it impossible for him to move anywhere or do anything. This is very effective and means that when the powers of darkness have been bound, their evil influence is cut off.

However, binding someone also implies that the bound one may seek to get out of his bonds as quickly as possible.

This is even quite natural. And in our battle against the enemy, we must expect that after every blow he receives and every defeat he suffers he will try to regroup his forces, change his tactics and try another counter-attack against us. That is the reason why in the prayer-movement we are working for the establishment of a permanent department of the Lord's army in every city, so that the binding can be repeated and upheld.

We are told by the Lord not just to capture the territory of the enemy, but also to keep it. Any good army would know that its objective is not just to win some significant battles. The goal is to win the war and keep the enemy out. There have been incidents in the history of warfare, where an army has won great battles but in the end lost the war. From the New Testament, in Matthew 16, we have already seen that binding is part of the keys of the Kingdom, and also that Jesus promises His Church that if we are in agreement we shall be able to bind powers in the heavenlies in such a way that they lose their impact upon earth.

There does not seem to be any biblical evidence though, that we are able to move great principalities and powers around from one locality to another, and I have already stated that this would not be of much help anyway. Casting principalities and powers out of this universe is not possible in this age, but we are able to bind them in their activities, and it seems to me that we do not need more than that in order to destroy the works of the devil. In terms of moving demonic beings we only have the one example in the New Testament of the Lord Jesus allowing some demons coming out of a man to go into a herd of pigs. However, we are here dealing with demons, not principalities and powers in the heavenlies. Demons are minor spirits, who are bodiless and who take abode in human beings. Principalities and powers are fallen angels with their own angelic bodies, and they do not inhabit human beings. Demons are meant to be cast out and commanded to leave, but not so with the territorial spirits ruling over geographical areas of nations and cities.

Pulling Down Strongholds

It is Paul who explains prayer warfare as

> '... *pulling down strongholds, casting down arguments and every high thing that exalts itself against the knowledge of God, bringing every thought into captivity to the obedience of Christ.'* (2 Corinthians 10:4–5)

It is clear from the context that this is a weapon that deals with the human mind being held captive through strongholds of false ideologies and philosophies. Strongholds of thoughts which are binding up people's intellect so that they cannot acknowledge God and believe in Him. This concerns strongholds of political, philosophical or religious nature. A typical example of this is Marxism, a political ideology, which for a period of time controlled almost two thirds of all people upon the earth. Even when it became crystal clear that Marxism was nothing but an illusion from the land of Utopia, multitudes of well educated and even intellectual people still kept clinging to it. This is because it was and still is, a satanic stronghold with arguments rising up against the knowledge of God.

Pulling down these structures in the mind of false thoughts and lies through the prayer warfare of the Church, means that we can destroy the demonic bindings and release people to be able to respond to the truth. This is what is meant by *'bringing every thought into captivity to the obedience of Christ'*. It is clear from this that this kind of prayer warfare is tremendously powerful in evangelism. Because it is not enough that we are able to preach the Gospel with power; we need also to be able to deliver people's minds from that which is besetting them and hindering them from being able to respond to and receive the Gospel. Many people are of the opinion that the reason for people's rejection of the Gospel can be found in natural causes such as a lack of understanding. But the apostle Paul explains that the apparent immunity in many people's minds is caused by the work of demons. Listen to these words from 2 Corinthians 4:3–4:

> *'But even if our gospel is veiled, it is veiled to those who are perishing, whose minds the god of this age has blinded, who do not believe, lest the light of the gospel of the glory of Christ, who is the image of God, should shine on them.'*

Knowing Our Enemies

Only a very bad army would get into a fight without a proper understanding of the enemy it is up against. Every army needs good intelligence information in order to know what kind of forces it is to battle against so that it can choose the right kind of strategy and the right kind of weapons. When that has been said, we need also to issue a warning against getting ourselves too focused on the powers of darkness. We don't need to know everything about Satan and his system of evil, just enough to be able to battle him successfully. Let us be careful not to try to develop a whole psychology of Satan by going way beyond the information we have access to in the word of God.

In the letter to the Church in Thyatira, the Lord warns us not to be among those who were deceived by trying to *'know the depths of Satan'*. The devil has been a deceiver and a liar from the beginning and he would very much like us to be misled into fantasies and imaginations of all sorts, so that by losing our sound mind, we can no longer discern the battlefield. Down through church history, many believers have ended their days in darkness and depression, because in their eager pursuit of the devil, they have lost their focus on the Lord and become trapped in false teachings and practices. Let us beware that our research is according to sound biblical principles and not according to occult practices.

On the other hand, we must also know what we are dealing with. Have you ever wondered why Jesus, on one occasion when he wanted to drive out a demon, first commanded the demon to disclose its true identity. *'What is your name?'*, was His question. In my understanding this procedure of Jesus throws a clear light on how the powers of darkness are working. The enemy's primary weapon is deception and disguise. Since he has already lost his real power through Jesus' victory on the cross, he can only try to bluff and fool all of us. There are scores of New Testament Scriptures that confirm this. The most common appearance of the enemy among God's people is that of an angel of light, and he has launched lots of religious demons against the Church in order to try and deceive her. This being so means that the exposure of the powers of darkness is a primary tool in defeating them. When light shines into darkness, the darkness dissolves; likewise when truth is proclaimed against lies, the work of deception is destroyed.

Paul, when he urges us to walk in the light and live transparent lives, says in Ephesians 5:13:

> *'But all things that are exposed are made manifest by the light, for whatever makes manifest is light.'*

Thus, we need to ask the Holy Spirit for illumination and discernment when we are dealing with the powers of darkness.

The Satanic Hierarchy

It is from Paul's words in Ephesians 6:12 that we have the most comprehensive understanding of the system of demonic powers in the heavenlies. All in all, we do not have much biblical explanation of the army of the adversary; actually we have very little. This is another indication that we should not try to build huge theological mountains on a small foundation. However, what we do have is the word of God, and it has been given to us for our illumination and instruction. My interpretation of Ephesians 6:12 is, of course, subject to my own imperfect understanding, and it should not be taken as more than that. Others may have other interpretations and maybe better ones than mine. However, we must dare to make an attempt to understand as much as we can of the enemy's army in order that we might better fight the good fight of faith.

Paul puts the powers of darkness into four categories. Again, I believe that he is speaking here about fallen angelic beings, not demons inhabiting human beings. We know that when Satan was driven out of the presence of God, out of Heaven, he was followed by one third of all angels. They were allowed to take abode in the heavenlies, which is the spiritual sphere right above the earth, also called *'the air'*. That's why Satan is called *'the prince of the power of the air'* in Ephesians 2:2. In this sphere of the air, the devil has established his government and is trying to dominate the earth. Since we also know that the devil is a created being, not being equal to God, he possesses no omnipotence. He cannot be everywhere as God, but is limited by his angelic body. Consequently, he must create a system of government with the group of angels that fell together with him. It is this system or hierarchy, that Paul describes in Ephesians 6:12:

> *'For we do not wrestle against flesh and blood, but against principalities, against powers, against the rulers of the darkness of this age, against spiritual hosts of wickedness in the heavenly places* (or high places).'

Principalities

The first category is called principalities. This word is derived from the word 'princes'. Since the devil himself is called *'the prince of the power of the air'* as we have already seen, the principalities must then be his second-in-command angels. These are the high-powered commanders in the army of darkness; those who are ruling over big areas of the earth on behalf of Satan. To me, the principalities represent the territorial spirits, of whose existence there is presently a big theological discussion going on in the Body of Christ. At the heart of the discussion is whether the concept 'territorial

spirits' is biblical or just a product of charismatic imagination. In my mind, however, there is no doubt that they are
a biblical reality.

First of all, one only has to consider what I already said
about the devil not being able to manifest omnipotence. This
means that if he is going to try to rule the nations (and
nobody with knowledge of God's word would deny this),
then, logically, he must appoint some of the most highly
ranked of his fallen lot to help him rule the different parts of
the earth and the peoples. Then, we can study the book of
Daniel chapter 10 verses 12–15, where it is clearly stated that
the opposition to Daniel's prayers being answered was led by
a demonic being called *'the prince of Persia'*, that is, the
spiritual principality which ruled the whole Persian empire.
And God's angel, who visited with Daniel, explained that
when he had finished with the prince of Persia, the prince of
Greece would come forth. And as we know from world
history: the Persian empire was overcome and replaced with
the Greek empire. Does this not confirm the existence of
territorial spirits to be a biblical fact? One must be spiritually blind to overlook such clear statements.

I have no doubt whatsoever in my mind that there are
principalities-in-charge over regions, nations and cities of
the world, and I believe that knowing more about their true
identity would tremendously help the Church in any given
geographical location to wage effective prayer warfare
against the powers of darkness and pull down their strongholds. To me, the key to this whole area is learning through
prayer to receive the revelation of the Holy Spirit. That is the
most important thing. However, I also believe that doing
research into past historical events – what is known as 'spiritual mapping' – can be very valuable, and help in detecting
the strongholds of the enemy. We have got to come to know
what we are battling against. However, let nobody think that
mere human research and knowledge can do it. We must
hear from God. We must wait for the Holy Spirit to illumin-
ate our hearts with divine revelation and wisdom. Because
the enemy is very tricky. His deceiving powers will do

everything possible to sidetrack us and lead us in the wrong direction.

Powers

This category can be seen as demonic powers not ruling over geographical areas, but influencing areas of morality, globally. The word 'powers', indicates binding abilities. I understand powers as dark angelic forces enforcing bondages upon large groups of people on a global scale. For instance, I see alcoholism as one such global power enslaving millions of people all over the world, and binding them to the rule of Satan in their lives. I trust we are all aware of the fact that alcoholism is not a sickness as many humanists claim. It is a demonic thing imposed upon people by the powers of Satan. The same can be said about homosexuality. To insinuate that God the Creator deliberately created some people with an unnatural sexuality, is a grave offense to the Almighty God. No, this is another 'power' keeping yet other millions in bondage all over the world. And so is drug addiction, of course.

In the days of the Jesus Movement, I worked in an evangelistic ministry that was reaching out to hippies and drug-addicts. In this ministry, we realized, only too soon, that we were not dealing with people that were sick in the natural sense of the word. We literally saw and heard demons every day, and if before that time I had ever doubted the reality of demonic bondages, then I was thoroughly cured from every shadow of a doubt through those five years of leading a drug-addict center in downtown Copenhagen. It was the reality of this 'power' that first taught me the great importance of prayer warfare in the work of the Church. Without that, we simply got nowhere, but through it we saw several young people being gloriously saved and delivered by the power of the Holy Spirit.

Rulers

The word 'rulers' indicates to us that we are dealing with controlling spirits. We have the 'powers' who are enforcing corruption upon the people, and we have the 'rulers' who are master-minding the ideologies and philosophies behind it all. The rulers are working to set up these ideologies in the heads of groups of people. There are political ideologies like Marxism, Socialism, Fascism and Capitalism. They have all proven to be useful instruments in the hand of Satan to control people and keep them away from God. None of the present political ideologies are leading people to God. They are all basically anti-Christian. The reason is, of course, that the *'whole world lies under the sway of the wicked one'* (1 John 5:19). All talk about 'Christian nations' and 'Christian politics' during this present age is an empty illusion. But God has a firm plan to change that, when he introduces His new world order and His Kingdom upon the earth in the age to come.

A real clear example of the work of the rulers is Nazism. It has become evident that Adolf Hitler as a person was nothing less than a medium for a demonic ruler, and his political ideas were not of human origin but deeply inspired by a demonic power. Many of us believe that he was completely in the power of the principality of anti-semitism, one of the most powerful rulers in the world today, which keeps millions of people bound in an unnatural hatred towards the Jewish people and anything Jewish. Even quite a few people in the world-wide Church of Jesus Christ seem to be under this ruling power.

There is absolutely no way that the bestial murder of six million Jews during the Holocaust could be explained as something natural. How could some of the most educated and spiritually illuminated people on earth, the Germans, fall prey to such a primitive and inhuman ideology as Nazism? Because they were deceived by the ruler of anti-semitism, and apparently even the Church in Germany was unable to discern what was going on until it was too late. As a person with German roots, myself, and who also presently lives in Germany, I can see two reasons why Germany was deluded by this ruler of anti-semitism.

First of all, because the Church in this nation had allowed

itself to be defiled with liberal theology. Actually, liberal theology and its brother, biblical criticism, was made in Germany. The fruit of this was that people were taught to no longer consider the Old Testament to be the inspired Word of God, but basically just the history book of the Jewish people and, in essence, mythical. In this way, the reality of God's election of the Jewish people and His ever abiding love for them was totally exterminated. The Jews no longer were the 'apple of His eye', but were reduced to an alien people that was, in effect, exploiting the German race.

Secondly, the Church in Germany joined the Evangelical church world-wide in taking a strong stand against the Pentecostal revival in the beginning of this century. And so, when the Pentecostal revival knocked on its door, evangelical leaders met in Berlin in 1910 and signed a document banning the Pentecostal movement saying that it came from the devil. I believe that this tragic action grieved the Holy Spirit and excluded Him from renewing God's people in the German nation. The German Church, consequently, lost the ability to discern spirits, having rejected the Holy Spirit who alone can give us the eye-salve that enables us to discern correctly. Therefore, the German Church was deceived by Hitler to such a degree, that except for just a handful of church leaders, it actually supported him.

Hosts of Wickedness in High Places

The reason why I prefer the old King James version here, using *'high places'* is that it gives me a better clue to the identification of this category. Some would say that I use it because it suits my theology better. So be it!

'Hosts of wickedness in high places' to me indicates that we are talking about Satan's department of religious or occult powers. 'High places' is an expression used in the Word of God to signify the practice of idolatry and witchcraft. It was common in times past – and even is today – that the mountains were used for the worship of false gods. The term *'hosts of wickedness'* indicates that we are here dealing

with those forces in the satanic hierarchy whom God considers to be the most wicked and the most dangerous. At least, for the Church. The whole contest, as it were, between fallen Lucifer and God Almighty is about who will get the worship from man. The devil was willing to give away all he had, the Kingdoms of this world and all their glory, if only Jesus, the Son of God, would fall down and worship him.

This is the ultimate goal of Satan: to steal all worship by creation from God. The sin of worshiping gods other than the only true One is listed as the most grave one of all. This is why this issue is dealt with in the first of the ten commandments, because it shows the priority it has in God's own heart. In order to steal away the worship which rightly belongs to God, the devil has a whole department of deceiving spirits assigned to operate within the area of man's religiosity. There are some who operate within the Christian Church to try to mislead and sidetrack, to cause division and theological strife, to try to make us fall from grace and give ourselves to legalism. Heresies, legalism, liberalism – anything that would lead us into extremes and draw us away from the truth of the Word of God. The field is enormous, and the devil seems to have had quite a bit of success down through the history of the Church. He will do anything to get us away from 'worshiping God in truth and in spirit'.

It is actually amazing how much these demons have been able to accomplish in terms of misleading God's people. The Church is full of dead religion, and its practice is a mixture of the Word of God and occult practices.

There are denominational churches in the world today that are using New Age material in their teachings and so are practising occultism in their ministry to the people. These wicked forces in high places are even sowing their poison into the Charismatic movement. Where it became accepted to let oneself be 'carried away in the Spirit' and not be careful to discern experiences in the light of God's word, the Charismatic church opened itself up to be fooled by religious spirits to practise many strange things, which, to me, look more like hocus-pocus than a life in the Spirit of God.

When the Spirit is over-emphasized at the expense of the Word, we are in danger of being manipulated by religious spirits.

In the same way, where the Evangelical, non-Charismatic church has over-emphasized the written Word to the extent of almost worshiping the Bible and swearing faithfulness to the written letter, instead of understanding the Word through the Spirit, the result has been a type of fundamentalism that is killing people and leaving the Church in the bondage of legalism. The hosts of wickedness are clever to exploit the situation on both sides. The desperate need of the hour is a balance and soberness of mind. We need both the Word and the Spirit in a balance of equality in order to avoid any extremes that, in turn, put us in danger of being infiltrated by religious spirits.

The occult powers of darkness also work in secular society, trying to exploit the religious desires coming from the fallen image of God in people. Today we are actually experiencing a forceful revival in the area of occultism.

The whole network of the New Age movement is a clear indication of this. People are being religious as never before. The emptiness of materialism is causing millions of people to seek after some kind of spiritual meaning and content. And the devil is there to exploit people's needs and feelings. He has responded to this need in a very clever way and has composed a very convenient and manifold offer designed to suit almost anyone. The network of New Age is his clever move. In there, you find everything in terms of beliefs. The great 'truth' ruling this cluster of occult practices and religious beliefs is 'peace and tolerance'. There is room for the Moslem faith, for Hinduism and Buddism, for Bahai, Scientology, TM and all the rest of the Eastern religions. Dead Christianity is also being welcomed. Only two categories of people cannot be included: the born again Christians and the Bible-believing Jews! They are both 'intolerant' people due to their faithfulness to the Word of God. Other than that, anyone can find a religious belief or occult practice that suits him. Through this great 'mixture', the devil is working hard to steal the worship from human hearts, which rightly belongs to the Lord.

The Objective of Prayer Warfare

To do spiritual warfare for the sake of excitement is senseless. Only trigger-happy people would have a good time doing that. Far too often, Christians lack the understanding of why they are doing the things they are doing, and when that is so, we are easily sidetracked and often end up wasting our time and energy on idle things. We must have a clear goal before us in order to be effective in our work.

Prayer warfare cannot stand alone, and it is also a bad idea when some people have left their normal life in the body to specialize as so-called 'prayer-warriors'. To be only taken up with focusing on darkness and evil and battling against it, without being a part of the constructive business of preaching the Gospel and building the Church, is a very unhealthy thing. We must have the wisdom to know the right place and role of prayer warfare as being just a part of the overall work of the Church. We must not fall for the temptation, as some already have, of thinking that spiritual warfare is the new answer to every situation and every problem. Because it is far from that! It is not even one of the most important aspects of the overall work of the Church. The calling of the Church is to be a testimony to Jesus and to preach the Gospel, to build the Church and to introduce the Kingdom of God in secular society. And as we are doing that with all of our heart we will often find that we are being hindered and opposed by the powers of darkness, who do not want us to succeed in the business of the Kingdom. It is when we are being hindered that we take up spiritual warfare to defend ourselves and to push away the powers who are standing in the way of the advancing work of the Church.

Quite a few Bible-scholars are of the opinion that Paul in Ephesians 6 is portraying spiritual warfare as being of a defensive nature. I have no problem accepting that, provided it means that we as the Church are very aggressively moving forward in order to build the Church and to introduce the Kingdom. After all, Jesus pointed out that the binding of the strong man was necessary in order to plunder his house and take out his possessions. The goal was to take the possessions, but the means was to bind the strong man.

The goal of the Church is not to do spiritual warfare, but to promote the Kingdom of God everywhere. The means to achieve this is sometimes, and maybe quite often, but not always, by spiritual warfare. That is why all intercessors and prayer-warriors must make sure that they are always closely joined up with the Body of Christ, fitting in with the overall work of the Church, and thus being just one group doing their part in the overall strategy and ministry of the Church. Where prayer warfare is being linked with world evangelism, with church planting and church building activities, with missionary work and social mercy-ministry, it becomes a very useful tool to promote the Kingdom of God on the earth.

Chapter 8

Put On the Whole Armor of God

Paul says:

> '... the weapons of our warfare are not carnal, but mighty in God for pulling down strongholds.'
>
> (2 Corinthians 10:4)

God has given us all that we need for the spiritual battle to which He has called us. It is all included in what is known as the whole armor of God in Ephesians 6.

We are, first of all, exhorted by the apostle to 'be strong in the Lord and in the power of His might'. We are not to fight the enemy in our own strength at all. That would be to use carnal weapons, and they are of no effect in the spiritual realm. We are also not supposed to consider the armor of God as something we can handle in the natural.

One hears about strange practices among Christians where they have been told to literally put on the spiritual armor. One such 'good' advice is to spend time every morning in front of the mirror and, in a physical exercise, take each piece of the armor and place it over our body. A kind of morning-aerobics. This belongs to the category that I call Charismatic hocus-pocus, because there is no way in which we are able to be clothed in the armor of God. If so, this would also mean that we should clothe ourselves 'with Christ', as we are urged to do in the New Testament, by putting Him on through a physical exercise every morning, just like we put on our clothes after the morning shower? What kind of superstition is this?

To put on the armor simply means to abide in Christ. Remember that we were told to be strong in the Lord and in the power of His might! And to abide in Christ means that we fulfill the conditions, such as confessing our sins and walking in the light, keeping our trust in the Lord, making sure that we are filled with the Spirit. The whole armor is Christ, He in us, and we in Him. It is as simple as that. To put on the different parts of the armor is the same as observing and obeying different spiritual principles for our walk with God.

Girded With the Belt of Truth

The first part of the armor is *'having girded your waist with truth'*. Now, Paul is, as we know, here portraying the armor of a Roman soldier of his time. To the Roman soldier, the belt was of the utmost importance as all the other major parts of the armor had to be fastened to the belt in order to be put on and stay on. In other words, no belt meant no armor. Also the thick and wide leather belt protected the waist, behind which life's most important organs, the kidneys, were hidden. The kidney's function is to cleanse the bloodstream from poison and uncleanness.

This, in fact, gives us a perfect picture of the most central principle of successful spiritual warfare. Without truth, without walking in the light, no weapon will be effective in the battle against the enemy. All our weapon-systems would fall to the ground if we were not clothed with the belt of truth.

Truth, here, is not truth in the sense of having the right and perfect doctrine. In that case, we would have but little hope of being able to fight the battle. It is truth in the moral sense. Truth as opposed to lies. Righteousness as opposed to unrighteousness. Honesty as opposed to pretense. Without the quality of moral integrity we can forget about being victorious against the powers of darkness. This becomes quite clear and logical when we realise that the very nature of the work of the devil is lies, deception and pretense. How would we be able to overcome the adversary if we have something of his own nature in us?

Paul has a very strong word to offer in this connection. In 2 Corinthians 13:8 he says:

> *'For we can do nothing against the truth, but for the truth.'*

The spiritual kidney-function is called *'walking in the light'*. We read about it in 1 John 1:7–9:

> *'... if we walk in the light as He is in the light, we have fellowship with one another, and the blood of Jesus Christ His Son cleanses us from all sin. If we say that we have no sin, we deceive ourselves, and the truth is not in us. If we confess our sins, He is faithful and just to forgive us our sins and to cleanse us from all unrighteousness.'*

What it speaks about here is a continual cleansing by the blood of Jesus taking place as we make sure we walk in the light. To maintain this cleansing, all we need to do is to confess any kind of sin that we might get involved in. That is what is meant by having your waist girded with the belt of truth. It is not moral perfection or sinlessness that is required. We are even warned against claiming that, for it is not true that we have no sin. Taking on the belt of truth is not done by some aerobic movement in front of the mirror, but is done by making sure that our sins are covered by the blood of Jesus and we are walking forward in the light.

The Breastplate of Righteousness

This piece of the armor of God covers the heart. The Scriptures say that it is from the heart that life goes forth. We need protection for our heart and, in particular, the part of our inner man that we call the conscience.

This spiritual organ of our soul is very sensitive and a constant target for the enemy's condemnation.

If the enemy cannot attack us on the grounds of having committed concrete sins, he will try to bring us under condemnation. He will say that we are not as we should be. We have not done what we should do. We have not prayed enough or read God's word enough. He will also try to remind us of past sins that have been forgiven long since. Condemnation is a very powerful weapon, and the enemy knows how to use it in many subtle ways.

Condemnation does not work only in the area of sins, it also works in the area of things that we have not been able to accomplish.

Whenever we suffer from a hurt conscience we become unable to fight in the battle. The breastplate is not covering our hearts.

To his young friend, Timothy, Paul charges to have *'faith and a good conscience'*. And then, he adds that some have rejected the good conscience with the result that their faith has been shipwrecked (1 Timothy 1:18–20). With a damaged conscience, we lose our faith and boldness and we are unable to overcome the powers of darkness.

That is the reason why Paul, himself, was very alert to ensure that always, in all things, he had a good conscience. *'I thank God, whom I serve with a pure conscience...'*, he writes to Timothy in the 2 Timothy 1:3. Also in his speech to Felix, as recorded in Acts 24:16, he says: *'I myself always strive to have a conscience without offense toward God and men.'*

What is it to put on the breastplate of righteousness? First of all, it means that we hide ourselves behind the righteousness of Christ. We confirm that we are in Christ and He was made our righteousness. We are justified by the finished work of the Lord Jesus, and there is nothing for the accuser to find. The Scripture makes it clear that there is *'no condemnation to those who are in Christ Jesus'* (Romans 8:1). The breastplate of righteousness is the righteousness of Jesus applied to us. This is a position that we must take and hold firm to, and not let ourselves become involved in trying to justify ourselves.

According to Revelation 12:10–11, we have overcome the accuser of the brethren *'by the blood of the Lamb'*. His blood makes us righteous before God and no accusation can hold against us. That is the breastplate of righteousness.

The Shoes of the Preparation of the Gospel of Peace

This weapon is about being ready and willing to preach the Gospel. To abide in Christ is not just standing in a passive position. It is also to obey Him. *'If you abide in Me, and My words abide in you... '*, Jesus said (John 15:7). Obedience to His word in preaching the gospel of peace is a powerful weapon against the enemy.

Spiritual passivity is actually very dangerous because it exposes us to the enemy and makes us an easy target. There is an old saying that the best defence is a counter-attack. It is always much more difficult to hit a moving target than a stationary one.

When king David fell into his great sin and became an adulterer and a murderer, the background had to do with David not being willing to move out into battle. 2 Samuel 11:1–2 tells us that when the time had come when the kings go out into battle, David decided to stay home and instead sent his general, Joab. Also, he stayed in bed all day and when evening came, he went out of his bed and entered the roof of the palace. It was then that he spotted the beautiful woman, Bathsheba, and most of you will remember the end of that tragic story. Had David gone out to do battle for the Lord as he used to do instead of lying on his bed all day, he would not have exposed himself to this attack by the enemy.

Jesus tells the story about the demon who had been cast out of a man. It then floated around seeking another house to inhabit but found none. It then discovered that its previous habitation was empty, cleaned and decorated, and so, it went out and found seven other demons worse than itself and they all moved in. What the Lord wants to emphasize is how important it is for us never to be idle and void, but always be filled with the Spirit and eagerly serve the cause of His Kingdom.

Our life with the Lord could be compared to running a race. And a race certainly means that we are on the move forward.

> '...let us lay aside every weight, and the sin which so easily ensnares us, and let us run with endurance the race that is set before us.'   (Hebrews 12:1)

Let us put shoes on our feet, being prepared and ready to preach the Gospel of peace.

The Shield of Faith

The shield of faith has a function of the same nature as the shoes. It is a movable weapon enabling us *'to quench all the fiery darts of the wicked one'* before they start burning against us. These darts are thoughts of anxiety and fear that the enemy is shooting into our mind. We need to learn how to quickly reject such thoughts before they begin to grow in our minds. Somebody once told me that God's people should learn to drown their worries instead of teaching them how to swim.

Martin Luther once said concerning our thought life:

> 'You cannot prevent the birds flying over your head, but you can prevent them from landing on your head to start building a nest!'

How true this is. We cannot prevent evil thoughts from being offered to us. Apparently, the Lord has allowed this to happen. Nobody can shield himself from being exposed to temptations. It is what we do with the temptations that matters. To lift the shield of faith means to take action against thoughts that are trying to hold on to our minds. All sin begins as a thought, a temptation in the mind.

So it was with Judas, who betrayed his Master. He had been given charge over the money-box as the cashier of Jesus and his little band of disciples. His tragedy started when he gave in to persistent thoughts about putting money into his own pocket. In doing so over a long period of time, without repenting, he was opening his mind and heart up, and when the thought was offered to him that he could get big money by betraying Jesus he could no longer resist, and he ended up being possessed by the enemy. Because he never reacted to these fiery darts from the devil they ended up by fatally wounding him.

When the apostle Peter exhorts us to resist the devil firmly in the faith, he gives us a practical example of how that can be done. He says that we should cast all our cares on the Lord, for He cares for us. The cares, the worries, the anxiety and the fears are fiery darts, and we have got to take action against them. Such thoughts can be likened to hand-grenades. If a hand-grenade is thrown into a house, you know that you will only have a few seconds to grab hold of the grenade and throw it back out through the window. Otherwise a big explosion will occur inside your house and you might be seriously hurt.

Passivity is the playground for demonic forces. The Danish Bible translation has an interesting version of Paul's words from 1 Corinthians 12, where he speaks about what it is like to be under the control of demons. He says in the first verse:

> *'You know that when you were pagans, you were carried away to these dumb idols without resisting.'*

The mark of being influenced by demons is that you are being forced against your will. You are passively allowing being dragged into the net. The Holy Spirit never works that way. He is a great respecter of our personal integrity. He would never force Himself upon us or do anything to which we would not give our free and willing co-operation. So, when believers claim that they were forced to speak in tongues or forced to give a prophecy, and that they could not hold it back, you know that they were not inspired by the Holy Spirit.

The basic principle for our co-operation with the Holy Spirit is this:

> '...the spirits of the prophets are subject to the prophets.'   (1 Corinthians 14:32)

That means that God wants you to be in control over what you are doing and not be like a spiritist medium that is taken over by outside forces.

Using the shield of faith means that we are taking action against whatever enters our heads. Paul speaks about *'bringing every thought into captivity to the obedience of Christ'* (2 Corinthians 10:5). That is using the shield of faith as a powerful weapon in the spiritual battle.

The Helmet of Salvation

Both the helmet of salvation and the sword of the Spirit are explained as being the word of God. In order for us to be able to keep our position in Christ against the attacks of the enemy, it is required of us that we know how make use of the word of God.

The helmet of salvation speaks about the more defensive power that God's word provides, whereas as we shall see later, the sword of the Spirit is the aggressive use of the word.

The helmet covers the head. That is quite obvious. For the soldier, the head remains the most difficult part to protect because he must also be able to see, to hear and to use his senses in the battle. The head, therefore, is very exposed to the attack of the enemy. This is a picture of our mind. The battle for the mind is raging.

When little David went out against the giant Goliath this was his strategy: to hit him in his head, knowing that this was the only part of this big man's body that could not be well protected by the heavy armor of steel. That is why we need to put on the helmet of salvation. The meaning of this spiritually is that however much we do to protect ourselves, we need to rely on God's grace and salvation, especially when we speak about the mind.

We have already seen that our mind lies open for the enemy to influence us. He does have access to our thought-life which we cannot prevent. We need the covering of God's salvation, to trust Him to protect us in areas where we cannot do anything ourselves.

It is true as Martin Luther said that we cannot prevent thoughts from entering our mind. However that does not mean that we cannot do anything to minimize this fact; to separate ourselves from the worst minefields; to withdraw from dangerous areas where temptations are particularly present. It is here the helmet of salvation helps us. We have in God's word a way of covering our vulnerable minds. We do this by filling ourselves with the word of God, by learning to meditate upon His truth, His salvation. Bible-meditation is a powerful way of filling our thoughts and directing our thoughts towards God's salvation. When we behold the finished work of the Lord Jesus on our behalf, it is as if we almost immunize ourselves against evil thoughts.

According to 1 Thessalonians 5:8–11, we are urged to put on the breastplate of faith and love, and as a helmet, the hope of salvation, and the blessing of doing this is that it protects us against depression. Thinking about what Jesus has done for us in saving us, thinking about the hope of eternal life is a helmet that enables us to be free of much discouragement.

It is exactly the same thought in Hebrews 12:2–3 where it says:

> *'looking unto Jesus, the author and finisher of our faith, who for the joy that was set before Him endured the cross, despising the shame, and has sat down at the right hand of the throne of God. For consider Him who endured such hostility from sinners against Himself, lest you become weary and discouraged in your souls.'*

What a powerful thing it is to meditate on the cross, to let your thoughts be centered around the work and the person of Jesus. That will keep us all from becoming weary and discouraged. That is what is meant by putting on the helmet of salvation.

The Sword of the Spirit

Take *'the sword of the Spirit, which is the Word of God'*. This is our weapon of attack. Actually, this is the only part of the armor that is meant for attack; all the others are defensive in nature. But using the Word of God under the power of the Spirit is also all that we need. The Word of God spoken in the power of the Holy Spirit was what brought the whole universe into existence.

We are here talking about an aggressive use of the Word of God, but not a mechanical quotation of Scriptures. We must remember that the sword is the Spirit's, not ours. It has to be the Spirit who operates the Word in order for it to be a powerful sword against the powers of darkness. That simply means that we are not talking about picking Scriptures of our own choice, but it is the Holy Spirit who gives us the Word that we use against the enemy. We call that a *'rhema'*, which is the Word spoken out of God's mouth for a specific situation.

When Jesus was confronted in the desert with the devil, He quoted the Scriptures against him and overcame Satan to such a degree that he had to withdraw greatly defeated. But this must not make us believe that it will work the same way if we just pick out Scriptures, any Scriptures, and throw them in the face of the devil. Such a mechanical use of the

Bible will prove ineffective. When Jesus went out into the desert and quoted Scriptures against Satan, it says in Luke 4:1 that He was, in fact, led by the Spirit into the wilderness, and He was filled with the Spirit as He met the devil. These same conditions must apply to us if we are going to overcome the devil with the Word of God.

Paul makes a clear distinction between *'the letter of the Word'* and *'the Spirit of the Word'*. And he goes on to say, that *'the letter kills'*, but *'the Spirit gives life'* (2 Corinthians 3:6).

There is no power or life in the written letters of the Bible. To believe that is actually to believe in magic. Paper and ink cannot accomplish anything. It is only when the written word has been breathed upon by the Spirit that it becomes alive and dynamic.

The revised version of the Bible has this very meaningful translation of an important Scripture concerning this matter, where it says:

> *'Every Scripture inspired by God is profitable for teaching, reproof, correction and for instruction in righteousness.'* (2 Timothy 3:16)

That simply means that we must make sure to let the Holy Spirit lead and guide us as we read the Scriptures. And as we move into spiritual warfare we must make sure to seek the Lord in prayer and listen to His voice in order to receive His *'rhema'* for each and every situation. Then, and only then, can the Word of God function as the Sword of the Spirit and cut down the enemy.

Chapter 9

The Prophetic Church

It was Moses who said: *'I wish that all the LORD's people were prophets'* (Numbers 11:29 NIV)! To be prophetic is of the utmost importance living in these last days. I believe God desires very much for His Church to be a prophetic Church. Being prophetic means to know what is important to God at a given time, and to be willing to be flexible and change according to how the Holy Spirit leads.

Far too often, the Church gets stuck in past blessings and traditions, and thus completely loses its awareness of where the wind of the Spirit is blowing. Again and again, we are warned in the New Testament to be on the alert, to be sober and watchful. The reason, of course, is that the enemy is seeking to side-track us from the center of God's purposes, so that we might waste our time and energy on things that are peripheral and without significance.

Jesus exhorts us to *'keep our eye good (that is; single)'*, so that our body can be full of light. For if your eye is 'bad' – that is diffused – your body will be full of darkness. What is the Lord getting at here? He is warning us against being diffused in our focus, side-tracked into many different things that are not in line with His heart and purposes. In a time like this, where confusion is great in the world we, as God's people, must have a clear focus in order to be in the light and to know where to go and what to do.

This becomes all the more necessary when we realize that

the enemy's deliberate strategy is to blur our spiritual sight and trap us into many activities that are without significance to the prophetic timetable of God in the days in which we live.

The book of Daniel gives a portrait of the situation during the anti-Christian period and describes the tactics and the strategy of the antichrist in his persecution of the saints. *'He shall wear out the saints'*, it says in Daniel 7:25 (RSV). The enemy is out to get us overburdened with activities so that we get so tired and worn out that we have no energy left to seek the Lord and find His way. This is why the apostle Peter gives us this warning in his first letter:

> *'The end of all things is near. Therefore be clear minded and self-controlled so that you can pray.'*
>
> (1 Peter 4:7 NIV)

This is what I mean by being prophetic: knowing that we are near the end and that God's priority for us at such a time is prayer. But sad to say, prayer is far from being the first priority in many churches today. This is probably because we either don't understand the time or we are so tired and worn out by other activities that we simply have no strength left for prayer.

It is also from Peter's first letter, chapter 5 verses 6–9, that we learn how the enemy seeks to pacify us by devouring us. To be devoured means to be preoccupied, to be overloaded. In the context we see that it is through the many cares of life that we are being worn out. That is why the Lord Jesus warned us against getting caught up with the cares of this life:

> *'But take heed to yourselves, lest your hearts be weighed down with carousing, drunkenness, and the cares of this life, and that Day may come on you unexpectedly.'*
>
> (Luke 21:34)

Watchmen on the Wall

Derek Prince, in one of his books, gives an interesting explanation of what it is to be a watchman. He says that the word 'watchman' in the Hebrew also can be translated 'secretary'. One could say then that to be a watchman for God means to be a secretary for Him. Derek Prince goes on to explain that a secretary normally has two main responsibilities. He has to know the agenda of his boss, and he has to remind his boss of all his appointments. As one who has had a secretary for many years I can only confirm this.

As the Church, we must know the timetable of our Lord and be in a position to work together with Him on His present day agenda. That is what it is to be a prophetic Church.

God is doing other things today than in days past. At least, it is true to say that His priorities are different than in times of old for the very obvious reason that now we live in the very last days of this age. If we don't know God's agenda, we are bound to waste our time and energy and also our money on things that are no longer important to God. Actually, it is my experience from 25 years in international ministry, that the Church world-wide is wasting a lot of time and resources in areas of evangelism, prayer, church building and spiritual warfare because we are unaware of what God is doing in the world today. We are therefore guided and bound by our past traditions and methods, just as if God had never moved forward since the days of our forefathers. How great the need is for the Church to be a prophetic Church that can flow along with God's present day purposes.

A couple of years ago, I participated in a prayer leaders consultation in the UK. Leaders from all the countries within the UK were present at the meeting, and they all gave a report of what was going on in their country.

When representatives from Wales gave their report I was quite shocked to hear that nothing much of spiritual significance was going on in Wales today. I could not believe it, remembering that it was in Wales that the last, great outpouring of the Holy Spirit had taken place at the beginning of this century. Wales was the birthplace of the Pentecostal revival in which I was brought up. When asked about the reason why Wales had become so spiritually barren, they said that the Christians in Wales seemed to keep looking back to the glorious days of the revival in the beginning of the century, and that nothing that God had to offer today had any appeal to them. They kept comparing everything with the former glory, and therefore, they were actually missing God in what He was doing today! Whenever this is so, the Church loses the spirit of prophecy and becomes useless for God's purposes in the world today.

What God is Doing in the World Today

I believe that the work of the Holy Spirit is concentrated around three major purposes that God wants to accomplish in the world in these last days.

First of all God's Spirit is working to bring the great commission to its completion. That is what we call world evangelization.

But we need to understand the issue of world evangelization in its prophetic sense. Otherwise we might waste a lot of time and money on the issue, because we have no end-time perspective, but only a traditional understanding.

According to Matthew 24:14 – the great end-time speech of the Lord Jesus – the gospel of the Kingdom must be preached in all the world as a witness to all the nations, and then the end will come. What we have here is something most prophetic. It concerns a matter that must be finished before the coming of the Lord Jesus. And since we are all looking forward to the coming again of the Messiah and want to hasten that day all that we can, this matter must take top priority in the work of the Church.

But we have to understand it rightly, the way that it is being expressed here. Jesus is clearly stating that He wants a witness of the Gospel of the Kingdom to be established in every nation (that is in every ethnic group of people) of the world. A witness implies more than someone just rushing through the land and proclaiming the Good News. It must mean that a church needs to be planted that can bear witness to the Kingdom of God in the land. The idea of just televising the Gospel into unreached places is simply not good enough. A witness in every nation to the reality of the Kingdom of God is more than just delivering some Gospel messages.

We have got to change our traditional ideas of world evangelization and line them up with God's prophetic purposes, and stop wasting time and money on this 'home-made' idea of mass-evangelism. If nothing is left behind after the work of the evangelist is completed, he has basically failed in his ministry.

Secondly, we are to establish a witness in every nation, not try to save the whole nation, which is not possible, anyway, on this side of the coming of the Messiah. God's prophetic agenda for the Church in these last days is to reach out to all the unreached tribes and peoples to establish a testimony of the Kingdom. It is not to 'Christianize' the nations. That has been tried before and it did not work. And those nations who were, then, proclaimed to be 'Christian nations' are today further away from God than any pagan people.

Christianizing the world is a like a figment of our imagination, an illusion that is sucking the Church of its energy and resources, which should have been used to accomplish God's prophetic purposes. The Christianizing of nations does not belong to this age, but to the coming of Jesus when His new order and His Kingdom will be established upon the earth.

Thirdly, the Church needs to make sure that the Gospel is preached and the Church planted in all the unreached nations first, before we go on preaching the Gospel and planting churches over and over again in our own nations. As one has expressed it: we must make sure that we preach at least one time for all, before we go on preaching a thousand times to the same few.

In this age, God has not indicated anywhere in the Scriptures that He expects all people to be saved from every nation. He expects a people to be taken out from every nation, tribe and tongue under the sun. That is the Church, and God's heart is burdened for that full number of Gentiles from among the nations to be gathered in. The idea that the whole world, meaning all human beings, would be saved before Christ's return is completely alien to the New Testament. Remember the apostle Paul's strategy for evangelizing the world. He started out with the Jews and he went around preaching the gospel to the Jews in the synagogues all over Asia Minor. But at a certain time, also due to the consistent rejection of the gospel by the Jews, he changed his strategy and began preaching to the Gentile peoples. Jesus wanted the Church to bear witness unto Him not only in Jerusalem, but in Judea and Samaria and unto the ends of the world.

The Lord does not want us to keep on preaching for ever to the same people who reject the gospel anyway. The disciples of Jesus were not told to do so. They were told that they should offer the Good News to people, but if they were turned down, they should brush the dust off their feet and go to someone else. And here we are in many churches today, trying so hard and investing so much in the attempt to evangelize the same hard-hearted, resistant people, when we could instead be using our resources to fulfill the great commission: to go to the unreached nations at the ends of the world!

Unity of the Body of Christ

Another area where the Holy Spirit is working hard is in the healing of the divided Body of Christ. The Scripture gives clear evidence to the fact that when Jesus comes back He will have a glorious Church to take unto Himself, a bride who has made herself ready for her Bridegroom (Ephesians 5:27 and Revelation 19:7).

In my understanding, a glorious Church can never consist of a divided people. Jesus said in John 17:22 that He had given His Church the glory that He had received from the Father in order that they all might be one. Thus, a glorious Church is a Church in unity, and a divided Church has no glory at all. Unless one believes that, in the end, Jesus will come and take unto Himself whatever is left of a miserable, divided, depressed and defeated people and that this will be His reward for His great suffering on the cross, then one must expect an intense activity from the Holy Spirit in these last days to prepare the Church as His lovely bride adorned for her Bridegroom. He is working in order to heal and unify the body of the Messiah and to beautify the bride of Christ.

Working for the unity of God's people in the cities and regions of the world is to work along with the Holy Spirit for the fulfilment of God's prophetic purposes in the end time. Thus, it is far more important to give our time and energy to bring forth the Body of Christ in its fullness in our locality than it is to work for the growth of our own Church or our own denomination.

Restoration of Israel

A third matter of great prophetic significance is the restoration of Israel as a nation to the ancient land of their forefathers. This is, indeed, a very prophetic purpose of God in these last days. In the book of Acts it says that:

> '... *heaven must receive* (the Lord Jesus) *until the times of restoration of all things, which God has spoken by the mouth of all His holy prophets since the world began.'*
> (Acts 3:21)

This simply means that the coming of the Lord Jesus is closely linked with the fulfilment of the prophecies of Scripture. If these prophecies are not being fulfilled, then the Lord must remain in heaven. I am sure we would not like that to happen. Therefore, we must, as God's Church, be eager to work on the fulfilment of prophecy.

One thing that was prophesied a long time ago by several

of the holy prophets was that, at the end of this age, the Jewish people who had been scattered to the four corners of the earth would return back to the promised land. They would come back and settle in the land, rebuild it, and it would blossom like a rose in the desert. Isaiah, Ezekiel and Jeremiah spoke of it, and so did several of the minor prophets. It would take up too much time to quote all the Scriptures related to this subject, and that is also not the purpose of this book. However, the biblical evidence is overwhelming. And it cannot be misunderstood or transferred into meaning the Church. The Church never did live in the land of Canaan. Nor were we ever scattered to all the four corners of the earth. This is clearly speaking about the Jewish people and, for them, these are historical facts. Therefore, it must also be them who are meant to return back to the land of Israel and be formed into a nation. How anybody can conclude that this has anything to do with the New Testament Church goes way beyond my good, logical, German mind.

And, also let me reiterate what was said at the beginning of this book that it is strange that those who spiritualize dozens of Old Testament prophecies about this subject, do not do this with all the prophecies. For instance, when the prophet Micah 500 years before Christ prophesied that the Messiah would be born in a tiny little town called Bethlehem, outside of Jerusalem, nobody would dream of 'spiritualizing' that. We all believe in the physical reality of it, and it has furthermore been proven by history to be a physical fact. But when the same prophets of old are prophesying that in the last days the Jewish people will return back to Israel and become a nation, then all of a sudden it is interpreted as a 'spiritual return of the Church'. It simply does not make sense, and besides, even in this instance we do have the physical and historical proof in front of us.

Over the last three years alone more than 700,000 Jews have arrived in Israel. God is bringing them back, because God is fulfilling one of His great prophetic purposes of the last days. For the Church to be a prophetic Church means that it involves itself as God's co-worker in accomplishing His plan.

The Present World Order

It is of utmost importance that we have a correct understanding of the present world order and what is going to happen with the world in these last days. Otherwise, this could become an area of much wasted time and energy.

As I said earlier, I do not think it is a profitable thing for us to try to 'Christianize' the present system of this world. Any attempt to save the world in the sense of saving the present world order, the present political system, is doomed to fail. We must not believe that we can save the world. In Matthew chapter 24, we are told by the Lord Jesus how it will be in the world at the end of the age:

> '. . . *you will hear of wars and rumors of wars. See that you are not troubled; for all these things must come to pass, but the end is not yet.*
>
> *For nation will rise against nation, and kingdom against kingdom. And there will be famines, pestilences, and earthquakes in various places.*
>
> *All these are the beginning of sorrows.'*
>
> (Matthew 24:6–8)

This is just one small part of the speech of the Lord Jesus, proving that in the last days the world will be shaken to pieces and collapse. Wars will increase and, believe me, not all the efforts of the nations and the UN will be able to stop that. Natural catastrophes will occur. Sickness will increase, and not all the prayers of the Church can stop it. Why? Because God does not want it to be stopped. He does not want the present world order to be saved. He does not want godless men in all their humanistic wisdom and strength to succeed. That would mean that the devil had succeeded in his rebellion against God, and that the tower of Babel finally had proven that man does not need God, his Creator.

All these ethnic battles as nation rises up against nation will increase until the world becomes totally unruly. When, thus, man's ability without God finally has been proven a failure, God will judge the world and introduce His new world order, His Kingdom on earth, where Christ, His Son, shall rule the nations from pole to pole. And then, only then, shall there be true peace on earth.

If this is so, why then should we waste our time and energy in an attempt to save a world that God has already long ago doomed to go under? Is this not what the Scripture means when, in two places – 1 Corinthians 7:31 and 1 John 2:17, it says that *'the world is passing away'*? The world here meaning, from the Greek, 'the orderly arrangement'. There is no hope of preserving the present political system governing the world, whether we talk about dictatorship or democracy. It must all be removed because it is all in its very roots anti-God and anti-Christ. For His Kingdom to be established, room has to be made for God's new world order.

However, that does not mean that the Church does not care about what is going on. We have already seen in previous chapters that the calling of the Church is to act responsibly towards all that God has created. But, in doing so, we do not believe that we can save the system. We are doing all we can to love people and care for people, taking our social responsibilities seriously, but for one purpose only: to bring them to a saving knowledge of our Saviour and Lord.

That is why, in the midst of this terrible uprising of ethnic hatred and war, we are told to bring the great commission to completion. It is as if this global ethnic strife can be exploited by the Church to get access to all the tribes and tongues with the Gospel and cause a great ingathering of people as the last revival sweeps over this world before Jesus comes again.

Revival and Apostasy

We are going to see a culmination of all things taking place in the last days. This is the correct translation from the Greek of Peter's words in 1 Peter 4:7:

'. . . the end (culmination) *of all things is at hand.'*

We need a balanced view of the things that will happen. Among Christians, we basically have two categories when speaking about the last days. We have the more traditional believers who expect the last days to be largely a time of darkness and apostasy. The majority of church members will fall away from the faith, and very few people from the world will be saved. We cannot deny, being faithful to the Word of God, that such a view does have support from the Scriptures.

The other more charismatic part of the Church claims that there will be a tremendous revival sweeping the world in the very last days, and that everything will be success and prosperity. Well, one cannot deny that we are still awaiting a global fulfilment of the prophecy of Joel; that the Spirit of God will be poured out on all flesh in the last days.

So, what is it then going to be? Judgment or Revival? The simple answer is both! Both a great apostasy and a great revival! Unless we, as the Church, receive both sides and preach both sides of the truth, we will not be able to prepare ourselves and the people around us in the right way. How we need prophetic insight and understanding so that we can be God's co-workers in His prophetic purposes and avoid wasting our time and energy on vain things!

Chapter 10

Rediscovering Grace

A couple of years ago, I had the privilege of attending a conference in Buenos Aires, Argentina. Part of the purpose of this conference was to give the participants an opportunity to come to know the Argentine revival and learn from it. It is probably true that South America as a whole, and Argentina, in particular, is the place upon the earth that has the strongest visitation from God in the form of revival at this time.

At the opening dinner, I was asked to sit at the head-table by Dr C. Peter Wagner, and as I got there, he proceeded to introduce me to the pastors sitting at the table in an unusual way. He said: 'You are sitting next to the pastors of the third, fourth and fifth largest, local churches in the world', and then he introduced me to the men. The number three in the world had a nice little church of 120,000 members in Buenos Aires. The number four had 'only' about 90,000 also in the city of Buenos Aires. The fifth was not from Argentina, but pastor of some 70,000 people in Nigeria. Then, I was told that the number two largest church was in Santiago, Chile, with 285,000 members. Only Yonggi Cho's church in Seoul, South Korea, was bigger. All in all, an impressive result from South America. No wonder that I kept asking myself during the whole conference about the secret of this unusual progress.

The answer came from Ed Silvoso, one of the leading

Bible-teachers in the Argentine revival: 'There are three pillars of truth behind the Argentine revival,' he said, 'the first one, being the most important, is that we have rediscovered grace. The second is what we called prayer-evangelism, and the third is unity among the churches.'

'We have rediscovered grace!' As I asked for further clarification of this, Ed explained that many in Argentina had observed over some time that the Western Church had become very legalistic as a whole and that this also had impacted the way in which they preached the Gospel. The emphasis was more and more on all the things people had to do in order to be saved, instead of an emphasis on all that Jesus had done for people's salvation. How true this is. We have fallen away from God's grace in so many ways without even noticing it ourselves.

A friend of mine gave me an example of this very fact. He had been working hard to get people in his city to come to a week's Gospel campaign in his local church. One evening, as he went out into the streets to invite people into the meetings, he saw a bunch of young people hanging around a street corner. One, who seemed to be their leader, had a beer in one hand and a cigarette in the other. Asked about whether he and the others would like to come to the church that evening, the guy firmly said no! 'I did it once before,' he added, 'but I just felt so bad, being constantly reminded of how big a sinner I am.' Just think of the difference if his impression of the church had been not about how great a sinner he was, but how great a Saviour Jesus is!

We do make an effort to bring people to repentance, but it is a question of whether we are doing it in the wrong way. Our constant call for people to repent is to require that which is extremely difficult if not totally impossible. No one can actually repent of his own choice. According to the New Testament, repentance is a gift of God. Jesus clearly stated that no one could come to Him unless the Father was drawing him.

When Jesus was evangelizing the woman at the well, how did He proceed? He knew very well that she was a sinner and even the details of her sin. She, of course, knew that herself. Did He go out bombastically exposing her sins from the start? No, not at all. He put before her a great offer of receiving living water so that she would never have to thirst again. Being stunned over such an offer her spiritual appetite rose up within her soul, and she said: *'Sir, give me this water!'* It was then that the Lord took up the question of her sins, but at that point, the woman was desiring God's gift so fervently, that she was willing to do whatever it took to get it. She had seen the grace of God; she had tasted His goodness.

It was Paul who said to the Roman Church:

> *'... do you despise the riches of His goodness, forbearance, and longsuffering, not knowing that the goodness of God leads you to repentance?'*   (Romans 2:4)

It is seeing and experiencing the goodness of God that brings people to repentance, not constant reminders of sins and going to hell if they refuse to repent. It was when Simon Peter saw the great blessing of the many fishes that came into their net through the Lord's word that he threw himself down at the feet of Jesus and said: *'Depart from me, for I am a sinful man!'*

Indeed, we need to re-discover grace in every way. Remember, we were saved by grace through faith, and not the other way round. Many preachers seem to indicate that we need to exercise our faith in order to receive God's grace, but that makes us saved by faith through grace, and that is altogether wrong. The truth is, that we need God's grace in order to have any faith at all to exercise.

Disarming the Principalities

It is an incredible thought and truth that the famous statement from Colossians 2:15 about the principalities and powers having been disarmed by the cross actually does not speak about territorial spirits in the world, but about spirits of legalism within the Church.

The cross completely delivered us from the law and set us free from the powers of religiosity, which are constantly trying to enslave us to observe the statutes of the law.

Paul is speaking about these principalities in the area of such trivial things as eating and drinking and observing certain days. He makes it as clear as daylight that we are completely delivered from rules and regulations in these areas. In spite of that, we see today how many believers are still in bondage to these things.

Concerning certain days, we have a whole denomination claiming the Sabbath on a specific day, disregarding both the work of the cross and the clear word of the New Testament. And concerning food and drink, we have a most strange set of teachings floating around in the Body of Christ. I heard about a certain area in a Scandinavian country where a group of churches had proclaimed the drinking of coffee to be sinful. I am eternally grateful to the Lord that He never called me to that place.

In another area of drink, we have a great dispute in the Body concerning the drinking of alcoholic drinks. One group of Christians who are strongly against believers having any enjoyment of alcohol, claim that the Word of God advocates a total prohibition, and have tried to prove that the word 'wine' as seen in the New Testament is really meant to be non-alcoholic grapejuice. First of all, they try to squeeze the meaning of the Greek to mean non-alcoholic, which, in itself, is a dishonest attempt to abuse the written Word of God. Then, they claim that the wine that was drunk at the wedding at Cana was non-alcoholic since Jesus would never change water into real wine. Obviously, they have forgotten to explain to us how on earth the people who drank of the wine at the wedding, could become drunk and merry from grapejuice? Also why would Paul warn us, not against drinking wine, but against being drunk, if the wine mentioned in the New Testament is nothing but grapejuice?

No, this is the work of spirits of legalism that want to rob us of the freedom we have from the law. Their commandments to us are:

'Do not touch, do not taste, do not handle' (Colossians 2:21)! Yes, it all looks so good and pious and Christian. That is the reason why Paul has this to say also from Colossians 2:23:

> *'These things indeed have an appearance of wisdom in self-imposed religion, false humility, and neglect of the body, but are of no value against the indulgence of the flesh.'*

It is of no value. It is self-imposed, not ordered by God. It is religion not true Christianity. It is basically a beautiful waste of time. And finally, and this may come as a shock; it is the work of demonic powers.

The overall principle for this is found in another word by Paul:

> *'All things are lawful for me, but all things are not helpful. All things are lawful for me, but I will not be brought under the power of any.'*　　　　　(1 Corinthians 6:12)

Somehow, it is important to the Lord that we live by grace. He has created us with a free will, with the possibility of making our choices, for which we, of course, must assume responsibility. He does not want us to become robots who are bound up by laws and regulations because that would greatly damage His own image in us. God has taken the chance of having us live by grace, of having the free will of choice. He wants it that way and He has taken the risk. There is no other way we can please Him.

> *'Stand fast therefore in the liberty by which Christ has made us free, and do not be entangled again with a yoke of bondage.'*　　　　　(Galatians 5:1)

Paul issues a strong warning to his young friend Timothy:

> *Now the Spirit expressly says that in latter times some will depart from the faith, giving heed to deceiving spirits and doctrines of demons, speaking lies in hypocrisy, having their own conscience seared with a hot iron, forbidding to marry, and commanding to abstain from foods which God created to be received with thanksgiving by those who believe and know the truth.'*
>
> (1 Timothy 4:1–3)

Notice that the falling away from the faith here has nothing to do with falling into grave sins. It is a matter of legalism, of giving in to commandments that are not from God. It is, in a way, about going further than God in some areas.

If the enemy cannot drag us into sexual sins, he tries to get us to abandon sex altogether and to consider it sinful in itself. In this way, we come to despise one of God's great gifts. If the devil cannot make us drink ourselves into the grave, he tries to make us abstain from drinking alcohol altogether and even despise it. His goal is to bring us into bondage so that we lose our free will and free choice. For whenever we come under the law and let the law direct our walk we come under a curse,

> *'For as many as are of the works of the law are under the curse; for it is written, "Cursed is everyone who does not continue in all things which are written in the book of the law, to do them." '*   (Galatians 3:10)

That fact is the reason why many believers are depressed and unable to experience the joy of the Lord. They have fallen away from the faith that is trusting the Lord for their life and way and have instead based their life on their own ability to fulfill the claims of the law.

But we have never been called to keep the law. That is altogether an Old Testament idea. Actually, we are unable to do it, no matter how much we try. That is why the law was not given to us in order for us to keep it. On the contrary, it was given in order for us to realize that we cannot do it and so that we would feel the need for a Saviour.

Paul expressly says that the righteous requirements of the law are not fulfilled by us, but in us, as by another person in us, namely Christ (Romans 8:4). For us, the focus is to learn to obey the Holy Spirit, and as we seek to walk in the Spirit, the righteous requirements of the law are being fulfilled in us.

True Holiness or Legalism

Today, there is a lot of talk about the need to be holy. The Church must be a holy Church. Maybe this present emphasis can be seen as a reaction to much carelessness and superficiality within the Charismatic movement, which has resulted in much carnality and sin.

Holiness is necessary. Anything less would be dishonoring to the Lord. However, we must beware that we are not, once again, in the history of the Church, returning to a bondage to the letter, to a fundamentalism, which is, in essence, nothing else but legalism.

Whenever the talk is about holiness in the Church, we always tend to focus on the negative side: all that we must refrain from, all that which we cannot do, all that which is forbidden. This was the whole idea about holiness that I was taught as a young Pentecostal. If I would stay away from smoking, from drinking alcohol, from going to cinemas and watching movies, and, of course, stay away from the girls, then I was considered a holy young man. What was important was what we were separated from, not to what or whom we were separated.

The word 'holy' means to be separated, but, of course, the major idea is that we are separated unto the Lord. If we are taking this avenue to holiness we would achieve a much better result. To be holy is, therefore, not to possess moral virtues or perfection, it is simply to be the Lord's through and through.

A good biblical example of this, we find in the story about

the rich young ruler. He came to ask the Lord what he needed to do in order to inherit eternal life. The Lord, then, mentioned six of the ten commandments as a requirement. The young man, being of a high moral standard, answered that he had kept them even from his childhood. Very impressive! We would no doubt have considered such a fine moral young man to be really holy. But was he in the sight of the Lord? No, for Jesus then added that he lacked one thing. Keeping some of the commandments does not constitute biblical holiness. He would have to sell all he had and give the money to the poor, and then come and follow Jesus. That, and that alone, is true holiness. To be the Lord's 100% and to follow Him with all of your heart. Unfortunately that was too much for this young man; to abandon his very life, so he went on being a good, moral, young man, but he was never a holy one.

God wants His Church to be holy, but not the legalistic way. He wants the Church to be fully consecrated to Him and to His purposes. That is the only form of holiness that is acceptable and pleasing to the Lord.

Chapter 11

Driven By Love

That leads me to my last chapter, and perhaps the most important of all that I have tried to say in this book.

God is not so much interested in all the things we are doing for Him as a church. He is much more interested in why we are doing what we are doing. What is it that is motivating our hearts?

Since we are children of the New Covenant we must learn, that everything has to come from within. We are not called to live by an external programme. We are not called to observe external statutes and ordinances. That all belongs to the Old Covenant. In Hebrews 8:10–11 the substance of the New Covenant is described like this:

> 'For this is the covenant that I will make with the house of Israel after those days, says the LORD: I will put My laws in their mind and write them on their hearts; and I will be their God, and they shall be My people. None of them shall teach his neighbor, and none his brother, saying, "Know the LORD," for all shall know Me, from the least of them to the greatest of them.'

The law is no longer to be observed from the outside as it were, but it has to be effected from within. We must be motivated, driven from within. What we do must come from our hearts, not merely from our heads. That is why so often we are urged to serve God with all of our heart. Just to observe some regulations from the outside is not enough, and it leads to religiosity. Everything which is not done from the heart is in fact nothing but religious exercise.

When the apostle Paul spoke to the Church in Corinth about being generous in giving help to the poor saints in Jerusalem, he expressed his desire this way:

> '*So let each one give as he purposes in his heart, not grudgingly or of necessity; for God loves a cheerful giver.*' (2 Corinthians 9:7)

This verse is the most commonly used Scripture when in the church we want to take up an offering. However we often use it to 'pressurize' the people to give a good offering, and in doing so we are actually violating the very Word of God. For according to Paul, God does not like anything that does not come from the heart, and He does not want to receive anything that is given out of compulsion. That is because God does not desire our money, but He desires the spirit of generosity and love coming from our innermost being. We cannot satisfy God's heart by just giving mechanically. He wants us to be motivated by our love for Him. Therefore we should rather discourage people from giving than trying to put pressure upon them. For whatever they give compulsorily has no value for God. It is just another empty religious act.

Paul uses the same approach in his letter to Philemon. Paul had led a poor man to the Lord. His name was Onesimus. And since Paul had to leave the place, he wanted his friend Philemon to take care of Onesimus. Listen how he approaches this case:

> '*Therefore, though I might be very bold in Christ to command you what is fitting, yet for love's sake I rather*

> *appeal to you – being such a one as Paul, the aged, and now also a prisoner of Jesus Christ . . .*
> *But without your consent I wanted to do nothing, that your good deed might not be by compulsion, as it were, but voluntary.'* (Philemon 8–9 & 14)

What a wonderful attitude there was in the old apostle. He did not want to use his apostolic authority, for he had come to learn through his walk with the Lord, that what is done out of duty and compulsion does not satisfy the heart of God. Only that which flows out from a thankful heart, responding to God's great love, is pleasing to the Lord.

Actually we cannot do anything worthwhile for God, unless it happens as a response to all that He has done for us. We must always have a fresh impression of God's great love and sacrifice for us in order to be motivated and respond to Him. The great missionary Count Zinsendorf found the great turning point of his life, when as a young man he entered that little church somewhere in Germany to pray. As he lifted his eyes in prayer before the altar in the church his eyes caught the picture of Jesus hanging on the cross of Calvary. Underneath the picture was this inscription: 'This I did for you; what have you done for me?' From that moment Zinsendorf was spellbound by the love of his dying Saviour and Lord, and that focus turned him into one of the greatest missionaries in the recent history of the church.

The Problem of Dead Works

In His great prophecies to the seven churches in Asia Minor, recorded in Revelation chapters 2 and 3, Jesus touches on the problem of dead works.

To the church in Ephesus His judgment is that the church had accomplished many good works and been patient in sufferings. But it had lost its first love. What does it mean to have lost, or left, the first love, whilst still carrying on with the good works? It simply means, that the works being done are no longer done out of love for Jesus, the Lord, but only as an act of Christian duty. That being so with the church in Ephesus, Jesus is calling the church to repentance. For God is never satisfied or pleased with just getting the job done. He wants us to be driven by love.

It is even more clear in the Lord's message to the church in Sardis (Revelation 3:1–3).

This letter to Sardis is supposed to cover the period of Protestantism in the history of the church. Reading the words of the Lord here with this thought of the development of Protestantism in mind makes a lot of sense:

> '... *I know your works, that you have a name that you are alive, but you are dead.'*   (Revelation 3:1)

This clearly is a precise description of the very mark of Protestantism: Nominalism! We have the name of being alive, but are in fact dead. The great majority of nominal Christians in the world today are Protestants. Somehow the great reaction to the over-emphasis on 'good works' by the Catholic church became 'empty works' among Protestants. That is why Jesus goes on in the following verse to call for awakening:

> '*Be watchful, and strengthen the things which remain, that are ready to die, for I have not found your works perfect before God.'*   (Revelation 3:2)

This speaks about the need for revival, and as someone so rightly has said, the history of Protestantism is the history of revival.

Jesus said that the works of the Church were not 'perfect' before God. This really means 'not fulfilling' to God. The word 'perfect' here can also mean 'filled'. In other words the works by the church in Sardis were 'empty' or dead. They were not filled with love for the Lord, but just carried out by way of Christian duty.

Being Nothing Without Love

Paul devotes a whole chapter in the New Testament (1 Corinthians 13) to tell us, that without being motivated by love all our effort and work is completely useless.

If we are able to speak with *'tongues ... of angels'* but have no love, we are nothing but *'sounding brass or a clanging cymbal'*. And if we have the gift of prophecy and know all mysteries, and all faith so that we can remove mountains, but have no love, we are nothing. Here is something for all of us faith-people or prayer-warriors to ponder about. If we are not doing what we are doing out of love all our ministry is reduced to some kind of useless fireworks.

Even if we are willing and ready to die for the truth, if we have no love, our sacrifice is in vain. Feeding the poor and burning your body in zeal for the truth is of no avail, unless you are driven by the love of Christ. We have got to learn that it is never our efforts that means anything to the Lord, but the underlying motive. It is not so much what we are doing that matters as it is why we are doing it!

Jesus laid down His life, not because He felt compelled to do so out of a sense of duty, but because He loved His Father, and because He loved us (John 10:17–18). His Father, our Heavenly Father would not have it any other way.

When Jesus restored His chief disciple Peter after his great fall, He renewed His calling to Peter to be a shepherd for God's people.

It is interesting to notice in John 21:14–17 what was the one great qualification Jesus was seeking in Peter's life. Three times He asks him this same question: *'Simon, son of Jonah, do you love me?'* He was not asking for any theological or philosophical education. Peter was a plain and uneducated man, but before Jesus gave Peter his great commission to care for His flock, He wanted to know where his heart was. When love for the Lord, our God, and love for His people, the Church, is flowing through our hearts, then God's heart is satisfied and He dares to entrust us with the responsibility to look after His sheep and lambs.

How strange it is today to discover that we are almost only interested in people's degrees of knowledge whenever we are out to hire them for the service in the church.

The Love of Christ Constrains

When Paul wanted to explain what it was that motivated him for his service unto the Lord, he used these words:

> *'For the love of Christ constrains us, because we judge thus: that if One died for all, then all died.'*
>
> (2 Corinthians 5:14)

In other words: the motivating force in Paul's life was the love of Christ flowing from the sacrifice of the cross, under which great impact he was constantly living.

The word 'constrain' has a special meaning in the original. It describes a strong current in a river. Paul's experience was that of having been plunged into a river and carried forward by its strong current. While living here in Germany I have tried to 'swim' in the river Rhein which has a very strong current. It was not much of a swim. All I had to do was to plunge myself into the water. Then I could lie still in the water and let myself be carried away by the current. I only had to perform a few strokes now and again in order to keep my direction straight. Thank God that the love of Christ is not a product of our own effort. It is God's gift to all of His true children. In Romans 5:5 it is expressed this way:

> *'... the love of God has been poured out in our hearts by the Holy Spirit who was given to us.'*

I shall never forget a true testimony to this fact about God's love having been poured out in our hearts by the Holy Spirit. In the beginning of the seventies I worked quite a lot in Sweden together with the leaders of the Charismatic movement. We had a real burden to bring together the spiritual leaders in the cities in order to promote unity in the Body of Christ. I remember I once heard about such an initiative in one city. A good friend of mine, being the Pentecostal pastor of that city, had called all the pastors together for a lunch meeting in one of the restaurants in the city. He had gone to great lengths in his efforts and even invited the Catholic priest, although he, as a Pentecostal, had much trouble even recognizing Catholics as real Christians. The turnout to the pastors lunch was almost 100%. They all came in time except two, the Catholic priest and my friend the Pentecostal pastor. As those two arrived a bit delayed all the other pastors had filled up the head table and there was no more room there. The waiter therefore directed the Catholic and the Pentecostal to sit separately at a small side-table. So there my Pentecostal friend was face to face with the Catholic priest. He fretted and asked the Lord for help saying: 'Lord, You know that I cannot stand Catholics and that I am not able to love this man sitting opposite me!' And the Lord replied: 'Yes, I know that you are not able to love this man, but how about letting Me love him through you?' My friend nearly fell off his chair by this surprising word from the Lord, and he hurried to say to the Lord: 'Oh Lord, would you really do that?' And before he could even finish considering this solution to his problem, he felt a hot stream going through his body, and before he knew what he was doing, he opened his mouth and said with a loud voice: 'Brother, I want you to know, that I love you in the Lord!' The Catholic man felt like someone had shot him between his eyes and he then broke down and started to weep. After a while he said: 'Nobody ever said to me before, that he loved me. You must have something that we in my church are missing. Could you not come to our church and tell us about this great love from God?'

And so it happened that my Pentecostal friend came to the local Catholic parish church and told the people about 'the love of God having been poured out in our hearts by the Holy Spirit who was given to us'. As a result of this meeting several Catholic people received the gift of the Holy Spirit.

The Last Revival is About Love

For some years now I have heard and have also been told, that the last revival before the coming of the Lord is the revival of faith. Although I can appreciate the great need for faith today in a Church which has fallen into apostasy in so many ways, I nevertheless have to disagree with this proclamation. I don't believe that 'faith' is the last offer from God. I don't even think that faith is the greatest need of the hour. I believe that 'love' is the greatest need for the Church. She must repent and return to her first love. This is the conclusion of that great chapter 13 of 1 Corinthians:

> *'And now abide faith, hope, love, these three; but the greatest of these is love!'* (1 Corinthians 13:13)

How can we think otherwise than God having preserved the best wine to last?

Also when you remember that the end of this age will conclude with the marriage of the Lamb, when the King of kings is returning to take His bride to Himself. And the Scriptures say that she, the bride, will have made herself ready. What else do we consider proper preparation from a bride than falling in love and being in love?

No, the last revival is about love, not about spiritual gifts and not about faith, but about the most precious thing, the eternal quality: love!

> *'... But whether there are prophecies, they will fail; whether there are tongues, they will cease; whether there is knowledge, it will vanish away.'*

But

'Love never fails.'   (1 Corinthians 13:8)

If you have enjoyed this book and would like to help us to send a copy of it and many other titles to needy pastors in the **Third World**, please write for further information or send your gift to:

Sovereign World Trust
PO Box 777, Tonbridge
Kent TN11 9XT
United Kingdom

or to the **'Sovereign World'** distributor in your country.

If sending money from outside the United Kingdom, please send an International Money Order or Foreign Bank Draft in STERLING, drawn on a **UK** bank to **Sovereign World Trust**.